THOMAS NELSON AND SONS LTD
Parkside Works Edinburgh 9
36 Park Street London W1
312 Flinders Street Melbourne C1
218 Grand Parade Centre   Cape Town

THOMAS NELSON AND SONS (CANADA) LTD
91–93 Wellington Street West   Toronto 1

THOMAS NELSON AND SONS
19 East 47th Street New York 17

SOCIÉTÉ FRANÇAISE D'EDITIONS NELSON
25 rue Henri Barbusse Paris V^e

SHAKESPEARE'S
TWELFTH NIGHT

Edited by
EVELYN SMITH, B.A.

THOMAS NELSON AND SONS LTD
LONDON AND EDINBURGH

Plays by Shakespeare in this series

TWELFTH NIGHT

PREFACE

THIS series is planned with one simple aim in view—
to make the reading of Shakespeare's plays as easy and
straightforward as possible.

Notes are reduced to the smallest compass. First,
in order that the reader's imagination may have definite material to work with, the Introduction gives
a description of the costume of the period ; and when
practicable, illustrations are given. Second, the text,
which is presented without any further preliminary,
is accompanied by footnotes which form a Glossary
of obsolete or misleading words.

The play may therefore be read at first sight without let or hindrance—without even the delay and
distraction which would be caused by turning to a
later page for such merely necessary explanations. But
there will be many for whom, if not at a first reading
yet perhaps at a second, something further may be
desirable—a bit of historical information, a para-
phrase of a difficult passage, or the clearing up of a
confused metaphor. To supply these, and to supply
them at the right time, is the object of the brief notes
placed immediately after the text.

Fourth, and last, comes a causerie in several divi-
sions : offering, for any who are studiously inclined,
a short commentary ; marking the place of this
particular drama in Shakespeare's career ; tracing its
importance in his poetic development ; estimating
its artistic value ; and suggesting a number of other
questions on which an intelligent student might reflect
with pleasure.

CONTENTS

INTRODUCTION

ENVIRONMENT AND APPEARANCE OF THE PERSONS OF THE PLAY

ILLYRIA has been identified with that part of Dalmatia, east of the Adriatic Sea, which, at the time when the events of *Twelfth Night* are supposed to take place, was under the dominion of Venice. It is likely, however, that the poet did not see it as a definite locality, as, in other plays, he saw Venice, London, and Rome. Like the enchanted island of *The Tempest*, and the moonlit wood of *A Midsummer Night's Dream*, it is a place of the imagination, and, like them, it seems as " real " as any actual place described by an Elizabethan traveller on his return to his native land.

The scenes pass from Orsino's palace with its music and flowers to Olivia's house of mourning and untimely revelry, from the streets of the city where there are " reliques " to be visited and Antonio and Sebastian lodge in the south suburbs, at the " Elephant," to the garden with the box tree and the sunny walk where Malvolio practises behaviour to his shadow. We may picture a sun-filled city on the Adriatic, with streets of white flat-fronted houses, with colonnades and arches. It is difficult to imagine that the room in Orsino's palace would be closed in : it seems near the violets of which he speaks ; and it may look on to a peristyle, between whose columns, beyond dark trees and tangled flowering shrubs, is seen the purple and emerald line of the sea, and its white shore. The room in Olivia's house where she receives Cesario would be closed from a view of the world outside. Her garden is of the beautiful formal Italian type which was imitated by English horticulturists, with straight paths, pleached hedges, and " knots " or flower-beds planted with bright crowded flowers. The main walks, or " forthrights," are enclosed on one side by a tall hedge cut into the shape of arches on trellises of carpenter work ; on the other side, at regular intervals, are planted box trees, trimmed into fantastic shapes. It is behind one of these trees that Maria tells her fellow conspirators to hide and watch Malvolio come across the letter, which she drops in the middle of a walk.

Here and there a touch of description suggests the appearance of the characters—the " red and white " of Olivia's beauty, Sir Andrew's hair, straight as flax, Malvolio's familiar smile, Maria's small stature and jaunty bearing ; and there are some indications of their dress and ornaments—Malvolio's yellow stockings and Sir Andrew's flame-coloured ones, Olivia's veil, and the jewelled miniature she gives Cesario, the steward's gold chain, and the branched velvet gown and watch of his day-dream, Sir Toby's strapped boots, and the general fashions of the " doublet of changeable taffeta," " gaskins " laced with points, and cheveril gloves. The names of the persons of the play are Italian and English, the general atmosphere suggests the same blend, and, as sixteenth-century English fashions, from the planning out of a garden to the cut of a doublet, were strongly influenced by those of contemporary Italy, the usual stage representation of the characters, with the possible exception of Viola, Sebastian, Antonio, and the Sea Captain, wearing either the Venetian or English costume of Shakespeare's own day, gives a picture which seems quite likely to be in harmony with that in the mind of the dramatist.

Men's dress of the period, either Italian or English, consisted of doublet and hose, shoes of leather or other

AN ITALIAN GARDEN

stuffs shaped to the foot, a ruff and a cloak. Colours were various and splendid, and our own age is not the only one which has distinguished " new " tints by fanciful names, for the silks and satins and velvets of the late sixteenth century were to be had in such shades as " lady's blush," " popinjay blue," " peas porridge tawny," and " dead Spaniard." The doublet fitted closely to the body, and, if in the Italian fashion, the front was cut into a peak. Rich black satin was a favourite material with young Venetian noblemen, who liked both doublet and trunk hose slashed to show a lining of some rich and splendidly hued stuff, or overlaid with a kind of lattice work of gold or some glowing colour. The " upper hose " were wide breeches or galligaskins (gaskins, Maria calls them), fastened to the doublet with tagged laces or points. With these were worn the " lower hose," or long stockings, often of silk, of a similar or contrasting colour. The ruff was large enough to balance the effect of the wide stuffed gaskins, which, without some such device, make the figure absurd. Rapier and dagger were worn, and the young men of Italy would carry a flower in one hand—a fashion which suits Orsino. Venetian hats were made of stiff silk or of velvet, with high crowns and narrow brims, or with no brim at all. They were adorned with a jewel, or a wreath of tiny flowers in metal work. Ornaments were rings, watches, brooches, and long chains, with pendants, sometimes containing a portrait. Malvolio imagines himself in his branched velvet gown, winding up his watch or playing with some rich jewel; but in reality, until he decks himself out in his yellow stockings, he is soberly dressed in black, with a plain gold chain and a staff of office. The fashion of cross-gartering was that of tying the garters below and above the knee—not of the crossed thongs from knee to ankle, fashionable at an earlier time, with which Malvolio is sometimes incorrectly represented in drawings of the garden scene. Sir

MALVOLIO

Toby's appearance is that of the bluff and jovial Elizabethan gentleman of middle age, who likes sport and a stoup of wine and a song, who praises the young woman he admires as a " beagle, true-bred," and abuses the man he dislikes as " a niggardly rascally sheep-biter." The " fashions of proud Italy " have little interest for him, and he might very well wear doublet and hose of frieze, of good cut, like that frieze jerkin of Sir John Harington's which won the approval of Queen Elizabeth, loose leather boots with straps, a small ruff, and a plain rather high-crowned hat with a feather. Sir Andrew appears as a " foolish gallant," his clothes a little " wrong," as those of such a character invariably are, colour an uninteresting green or yellow, ruff not set stiffly enough, slops or gaskins not stuffed to the proper proportion, cloak worn without the right jaunty gallantry—just the opposite, in fact, to Orlando when Rosalind tells him that he is " point-device in his accoutrements." Olivia's household should be in mourning. Fabian's black doublet is cut very simply, his ruff is small, his upper hose not padded out to the round shape, and his lower hose gartered above the knee. The jester did not always wear the distinctive dress of the " pied ninny," with deep collar and jerkin cut into points and hung with bells, but most people like to picture Feste in the garb so appropriate to his calling. He may wear magpie motley of black and white. This mourning scheme is not always followed on the stage, but one imagines that Olivia, who likes " shows of grief," might well have adopted it, and it is in effective contrast with the atmosphere of flowers and music, with their suggestion of colour, in Orsino's court.

Olivia's dress is made with pointed bodice, puffed sleeves, ruff, and skirt cut wide enough to hang in folds. A richly wrought girdle is fastened in front of the dress, reaching to the hem. Her long veil hangs from the back of her head, and she does not draw it across her face until Cesario approaches. Both dress and veil are black. Maria's black gown, of some sort of woollen stuff, is in the fashion of the time in its unexaggerated form—small ruff, tight bodice, wide skirt—and she wears a narrow apron and a handkerchief of silk or fine linen bound over her head. Olivia calls her "my gentlewoman," but the two do not seem on the footing of equal companionship, as are Portia and Nerissa in *The Merchant of Venice*.

When Viola is carried in from the wrecked ship she is enveloped in a "lap-mantle," a cloak made to cover the entire figure. As Knight says, the two sea-captains may very well wear "the picturesque habits of Chimariot, Illyrian, and dark Suliote," which Byron admired—

> "O ! who is more brave than a dark Suliote,
> In his snowy camese and his shaggy capote ? "

The characteristics of the dress are the shirt of soft white stuff, the zouave jacket, sash, loose white Turkish trousers reaching just below the knee, greaves, and scarlet fez. A similar costume is sometimes worn by Sebastian of Messaline and his sister, with, in place of the loose trousers, a short kilted tunic of white material. An advantage of picturing them dressed in this way is that, in the soft wide kilted tunic, the figures of brother and sister seem to be more alike than when they appear in the doublet and hose of Italian or English youth. Viola says that in the disguise she procures with the help of the sea captain she imitates the "fashion, colour, ornament" of Sebastian's dress, and we must believe, of course, that

> "An apple, cleft in two, is not more twin
> Than these two creatures."

As Viola certainly is not masculine (see page 29), Sebastian must be rather girlish in appearance—but in appearance alone, as poor Sir Andrew finds to his cost.

THE OPENING OF THE PLAY

Orsino, the Duke of Illyria, is passionately in love with the beautiful Countess Olivia, who, on the death of her brother, has made a vow to spend seven years in seclusion. Viola, wrecked on the coast of Illyria, not knowing if her brother Sebastian, with whom she was travelling, is alive or dead, disguises herself as a page and enters the service of the Duke. He sends her to Olivia to plead his cause, and the ensuing complications form the main part of the story of the play.

PERSONS OF THE PLAY

ORSINO, *Duke of Illyria.*
SEBASTIAN, *brother to Viola.*
ANTONIO, *a sea captain, friend to Sebastian.*
A Sea Captain, *rescuer of Viola.*
VALENTINE ⎱ *gentlemen attending on the Duke.*
CURIO ⎰
SIR TOBY BELCH, *uncle to Olivia.*
SIR ANDREW AGUECHEEK.
MALVOLIO, *steward to Olivia.*
FABIAN, *servant to Olivia.*
FESTE, *Olivia's fool.*
OLIVIA, *a rich Countess.*
VIOLA, *sister to Sebastian, during part of the play dis-
    guised as the page Cesario.*
MARIA, *Olivia's attendant.*

Lords, a Priest, Sailors, Officers, Musicians, and Attendants.

Scene : A city in Illyria, and the sea-coast near it.

TWELFTH NIGHT

OR, WHAT YOU WILL

ACT I

SCENE I

A room in the DUKE'S *palace.*

[*Enter* DUKE, CURIO, *and other* Lords ;
Musicians *attending.*]

Duke. If music be the food of love, play on ;
Give me excess of it, that, surfeiting,
The appetite may sicken, and so die.
That strain again ! it had a dying fall :
O, it came o'er my ear like the sweet sound
That breathes upon a bank of violets,
Stealing and giving odour !   Enough ; no more :
'Tis not so sweet now as it was before.
O spirit of love ! how quick and fresh art thou,
10 That, notwithstanding thy capacity
Receiveth as the sea, nought enters there,
Of what validity and pitch soe'er,
But falls into abatement and low price,
Even in a minute : so full of shapes is fancy

4. *Fall,* Cadence in music.
5–7. " *O, it . . . odour.*"   Of these lines Hazlitt says—" Shakespeare
   alone could describe the effect of his own poetry."
9. *Quick,* Alive.   12. *Validity,* Value.
12. *Pitch,* Standard of excellence. Technically, the height to
   which the falcon soars.
13. *Abatement,* Depreciation, *i.e.* falling in value.

19

That it alone is high fantastical.

   Cur. Will you go hunt, my lord ?

   Duke.   What, Curio ?

   Cur. The hart.

   Duke. Why, so I do, the noblest that I have :

O, when mine eyes did see Olivia first,

20 Methought she purged the air of pestilence !

That instant was I turn'd into a hart ;

And my desires, like fell and cruel hounds,

E'er since pursue me.

[Enter Valentine.]

                     How now ! what news from her ?

   Val. So please my lord, I might not be admitted ;

But from her handmaid do return this answer :

The element itself, till seven years' heat,

Shall not behold her face at ample view ;

But, like a cloistress, she will veiled walk

And water once a day her chamber round

30 With eye-offending brine : all this to season

A brother's dead love, which she would keep fresh

And lasting in her sad remembrance.

   Duke. O, she that hath a heart of that fine frame

To pay this debt of love but to a brother,

How will she love, when the rich golden shaft

Hath kill'd the flock of all affections else

That live in her ; when liver, brain and heart,

These sovereign thrones, are all supplied, and fill'd

Her sweet perfections with one self king !

40 Away before me to sweet beds of flowers :

Love-thoughts lie rich when canopied with bowers.

[Exeunt.

---

15. *Fantastical,* Imaginative.   21. *Hart . . . hounds.* See page 128.

22. *Fell,* Fierce.

26. *Element,* Sky. The word comes to be used specially of one
     element—the air and sky. See page 43.

32. *Remembrance,* pronounced re-mem-ber-ance.

35. *Golden shaft.* See page 128.

39. *Perfections :* pronounce four syllables.   39. *Self,* Self-same.

20

SCENE II

The sea-coast.

[*Enter* VIOLA, *a* Captain, *and* Sailors.]

Vio. What country, friends, is this ?
Cap. This is Illyria, lady.
Vio. And what should I do in Illyria ?
My brother he is in Elysium.
Perchance he is not drown'd : what think you,
      sailors ?
   Cap. It is perchance that you yourself were saved.
   Vio. O my poor brother ! and so perchance may
      he be.
   Cap. True, madam : and, to comfort you with
      chance,
Assure yourself, after our ship did split,
10 When you and those poor number saved with you
Hung on our driving boat, I saw your brother,
Most provident in peril, bind himself,
Courage and hope both teaching him the practice,
To a strong mast that lived upon the sea ;
Where, like Arion on the dolphin's back,
I saw him hold acquaintance with the waves
So long as I could see.
   Vio. For saying so, there's gold :
Mine own escape unfoldeth to my hope,
20 Whereto thy speech serves for authority,
The like of him.   Know'st thou this country ?
   Cap. Ay, madam, well ; for I was bred and born
Not three hours' travel from this very place.
   Vio. Who governs here ?
   Cap. A noble duke, in nature as in name.

4. *Elysium.*   See page 128.   11. *Driving*, Drifting.
              15. *Arion.*   See page 129.

Vio. What is his name ?

Cap. Orsino.

Vio. Orsino ! I have heard my father name him :
He was a bachelor then.

30   *Cap.* And so is now, or was so very late ;
For but a month ago I went from hence,
And then 't was fresh in murmur,—as, you know
What great ones do the less will prattle of,—
That he did seek the love of fair Olivia.

Vio. What's she ?

Cap. A virtuous maid, the daughter of a count
That died some twelvemonth since, then leaving her
In the protection of his son, her brother,
Who shortly also died : for whose dear love,
40 They say, she hath abjured the company
And sight of men.

Vio.   O that I served that lady
And might not be delivered to the world,
Till I had made mine own occasion mellow
What my estate is !

Cap.   That were hard to compass ;
Because she will admit no kind of suit,
No, not the duke's.

Vio. There is a fair behaviour in thee, captain ;
And though that nature with a beauteous wall
Doth oft close in pollution, yet of thee
50 I will believe thou hast a mind that suits
With this thy fair and outward character.
I prithee, and I'll pay thee bounteously,
Conceal me what I am, and be my aid
For such disguise as haply shall become
The form of my intent.   I'll serve this duke :
Thou shalt present me as an eunuch to him :
It may be worth thy pains ; for I can sing
And speak to him in many sorts of music

40. *Abjured*, Renounced.   42. *Delivered*, Made known.
43. *Occasion*, Suitable opportunity, right time.
44. *Estate*, Rank.   44. *Compass*, Bring about.

That will allow me very worth his service.
60 What else may hap to time I will commit ;
   Only shape thou thy silence to my wit.
      Cap. Be you his eunuch, and your mute I'll be :
   When my tongue blabs, then let mine eyes not see.
      Vio. I thank thee : lead me on.   [*Exeunt.*

SCENE III

A room in OLIVIA'S *house.*

[*Enter* SIR TOBY BELCH *and* MARIA.]

Sir To. What a plague means my niece, to take the death of her brother thus ? I am sure care's an enemy to life.

Mar. By my troth, Sir Toby, you must come in earlier o' nights : your cousin, my lady, takes great exceptions to your ill hours.

Sir To. Why, let her except, before excepted.

Mar. Ay, but you must confine yourself within the modest limits of order.

10 *Sir To.* Confine ! I'll confine myself no finer than I am : these clothes are good enough to drink in ; and so be these boots too : an they be not, let them hang themselves in their own straps.

Mar. That quaffing and drinking will undo you : I heard my lady talk of it yesterday ; and of a foolish knight that you brought in one night here to be her wooer.

Sir To. Who, Sir Andrew Aguecheek ?

Mar. Ay, he.

20 *Sir To.* He's as tall a man as any's in Illyria.

---

59. *Allow me*, Approve me, show me.
5. *Cousin*, used to denote any relationship except the nearest.
7. *Except, before excepted*, reminiscent of a legal phrase. **Sir Toby**
    makes such allusions for the sake of punning.
12. *An*, If.   20. *Tall*, Valiant.

23

Mar. What's that to the purpose ?

Sir To. Why, he has three thousand ducats a year.

Mar. Ay, but he'll have but a year in all these ducats : he's a very fool and a prodigal.

Sir To. Fie ! that you'll say so ! he plays o' the viol-de-gamboys, and speaks three or four languages word for word without book, and hath all the good gifts of nature.

Mar. He hath indeed, almost natural : for besides
30 that he's a fool, he's a great quarreller ; and but that he hath the gift of a coward to allay the gust he hath in quarrelling, 'tis thought among the prudent he would quickly have the gift of a grave.

Sir To. By this hand, they are scoundrels and substractors that say so of him. Who are they ?

Mar. They that add, moreover, he's drunk nightly in your company.

Sir To. With drinking healths to my niece : I'll drink to her as long as there is a passage in my throat
40 and drink in Illyria : he's a coward and a coystrill that will not drink to my niece till his brains turn o' the toe like a parish-top. What, wench ! Castiliano vulgo ! for here comes Sir Andrew Agueface.

[*Enter* Sir Andrew Aguecheek.]

Sir And. Sir Toby Belch ! how now, Sir Toby Belch !

Sir To. Sweet Sir Andrew !

Sir And. Bless you, fair shrew.

Mar. And you too, sir.

---

22. *Ducat*, Coin at that time worth 6s. 8d. in England.
26. *Viol-de-gamboys*, Bass viol.   31. *Gust*, taste.
40. *Coystrill*. Mean-spirited fellow.
42. *Parish-top*. A large top was kept in every parish to provide people with exercise in wintry weather.
42. *Castiliano vulgo*. Castiliano (Sp. *Castellano*, belonging to Castile) occurs pretty frequently in Elizabethan conversation as a slangy exclamation. For emendation of " vulgo " see page 144. But Sir Toby's foreign phrases are often mere nonsense—as are those of similar humorists of to-day.

50 *Sir To.* Accost, Sir Andrew, accost.

Sir And. What's that?

Sir To. My niece's chambermaid.

Sir And. Good Mistress Accost, I desire better acquaintance.

Mar. My name is Mary, sir.

Sir And. Good Mistress Mary Accost,—

Sir To. You mistake, knight: "accost" is front her, board her, woo her, assail her.

Sir And. By my troth, I would not undertake her in this company. Is that the meaning of "accost"?

60 *Mar.* Fare you well, gentlemen.

Sir To. An thou let part so, Sir Andrew, would thou mightst never draw sword again.

Sir And. An you part so, mistress, I would I might never draw sword again. Fair lady, do you think you have fools in hand?

Mar. Sir, I have not you by the hand.

Sir And. Marry, but you shall have: and here's my hand.

Mar. Now, sir, "thought is free": I pray you, 70 bring your hand to the buttery-bar and let it drink.

Sir And. Wherefore, sweet-heart? what's your metaphor?

Mar. It's dry, sir.

Sir And. Why, I think so: I am not such an ass but I can keep my hand dry. But what's your jest?

Mar. A dry jest, sir.

Sir And. Are you full of them?

Mar. Ay, sir, I have them at my fingers' ends: marry, now I let go your hand, I am barren. [*Exit.*

67. *Marry*, A mild oath (By *Mary*).
69. *Thought is free*, A proverbial expression.
70. *Buttery-bar.* The *buttery* was a storeroom for keeping food and drink, with a half-door over which these were served. The *buttery-bar* was the ledge on the top of this door, for holding tankards.
75. *Dry.* A dry hand was supposed to be the sign of a non-amorous disposition.

80 *Sir To.* O knight, thou lackest a cup of canary when did I see thee so put down?

Sir And. Never in your life, I think; unless you see canary put me down. Methinks sometimes I have no more wit than a Christian or an ordinary man has: but I am a great eater of beef and I believe that does harm to my wit.

Sir To. No question.

Sir And. An I thought that, I'ld forswear it. I'll ride home to-morrow, Sir Toby.

90 *Sir To.* Pourquoi, my dear knight?

Sir And. What is " pourquoi "? do or not do? I would I had bestowed that time in the tongues that I have in fencing, dancing and bear-baiting: O, had I but followed the arts!

Sir To. Then hadst thou had an excellent head of hair.

Sir And. Why, would that have mended my hair?

Sir To. Past question; for thou seest it will not curl by nature.

100 *Sir And.* But it becomes me well enough, does't not?

Sir To. Excellent; it hangs like flax on a distaff.

Sir And. Faith, I'll home to-morrow, Sir Toby: your niece will not be seen; or if she be, it's four to one she'll none of me: the count himself here hard by woos her.

Sir To. She'll none o' the count: she'll not match above her degree, neither in estate, years, nor wit; I have heard her swear't. Tut, there's life in't, man.

110 *Sir And.* I'll stay a month longer. I am a fellow o' the strangest mind i' the world; I delight in masques and revels sometimes altogether.

Sir To. Art thou good at these kickshawses, knight?

88. *Forswear it*, Renounce it.
112. *Revels*, special term for the entertainments given by the Inns of Court, of which *Twelfth Night* itself was one (see page 110).
113. *Kickshawses*, Trifles.

Sir And. As any man in Illyria, whatsoever he be, under the degree of my betters; and yet I will not compare with an old man.

Sir To. What is thy excellence in a galliard, knight?

Sir And. Faith, I can cut a caper.

Sir To. And I can cut the mutton to't.

120 *Sir And.* And I think I have the back-trick simply as strong as any man in Illyria.

Sir To. Wherefore are these things hid? wherefore have these gifts a curtain before 'em? are they like to take dust, like Mistress Mall's picture? why dost thou not go to church in a galliard and come home in a coranto? My very walk should be a jig. What dost thou mean? Is it a world to hide virtues in? I did think, by the excellent constitution of thy leg, it was formed under the star of a galliard.

130 *Sir And.* Ay, 'tis strong, and it does indifferent well in a flame-coloured stock. Shall we set about some revels?

Sir To. What shall we do else? were we not born under Taurus?

Sir And. Taurus! That's sides and heart.

Sir To. No, sir; it is legs and thighs. Let me see thee caper: ha! higher: ha, ha! excellent!

[Exeunt.

117. *Galliard,* A quick lively dance, "full of tricks and turns." One of these tricks was the *capriole,* the *caper* which Sir Andrew can cut, which "consisted in beating the feet together in the air."
120. *Back-trick,* A caper backwards in dancing.
123. *Curtain,* used to protect a valuable picture. *Cf.* Olivia's metaphor on page 36.
124. *Mistress Mall.* Perhaps "Moll Cutpurse," a notorious thief, often alluded to, and once or twice represented on the seventeenth century stage.
126. *Coranto,* A swift, lively dance.
134. *Taurus.* According to the teaching of astrology, each sign of the zodiac controls a part of the human body and affections. Taurus governs the neck and heart.

27

SCENE IV

A room in the DUKE'S *palace.*

[*Enter* VALENTINE, *and* VIOLA *in man's attire.*]

Val. If the duke continue these favours towards
you, Cesario, you are like to be much advanced : he
hath known you but three days, and already you are
no stranger.

Vio. You either fear his humour or my negligence,
that you call in question the continuance of his love :
is he inconstant, sir, in his favours ?

Val. No, believe me.

Vio. I thank you.   Here comes the count.

[*Enter* DUKE, CURIO, *and* Attendants.]

10   *Duke.* Who saw Cesario, ho ?

Vio. On your attendance, my lord ; here.

Duke. Stand you a while aloof.   Cesario,
Thou know'st no less but all ; I have unclasp'd
To thee the book even of my secret soul :
Therefore, good youth, address thy gait unto her ;
Be not denied access, stand at her doors,
And tell them, there thy fixed foot shall grow
Till thou have audience.

Vio.   Sure, my noble lord,
If she be so abandon'd to her sorrow
20 As it is spoke, she never will admit me.

Duke. Be clamorous and leap all civil bounds
Rather than make unprofited return.

Vio. Say I do speak with her, my lord, what then ?

Duke. O, then unfold the passion of my love,
Surprise her with discourse of my dear faith :
It shall become thee well to act my woes ;
She will attend it better in thy youth

5. *Humour*, Caprice.   21. *Civil bounds*, The limits
   of good manners.   25. *Dear*, Heartfelt.

28

Than in a nuncio of more grave aspect.

Vio. I think not so, my lord.

Duke.   Dear lad, believe it ;
30 For they shall yet belie thy happy years,
That say thou art a man : Diana's lip
Is not more smooth and rubious ; thy small pipe
Is as the maiden's organ, shrill and sound,
And all is semblative a woman's part.
I know thy constellation is right apt
For this affair.   Some four or five attend him ;
All, if you will ; for I myself am best
When least in company.   Prosper well in this,
And thou shalt live as freely as thy lord,
40 To call his fortunes thine.

Vio.   I'll do my best
To woo your lady : [*Aside*] yet, a barful strife !
Whoe'er I woo, myself would be his wife.   [*Exeunt.*

SCENE V

A room in Olivia's house.

[*Enter* MARIA *and* CLOWN.]

Mar. Nay, either tell me where thou hast been, or I
will not open my lips so wide as a bristle may enter in
way of thy excuse : my lady will hang thee for thy
absence.

Clo. Let her hang me : he that is well hanged in this
world needs to fear no colours.

Mar. Make that good.

Clo. He shall see none to fear.

Mar. A good lenten answer : I can tell thee where
10 that saying was born, of " I fear no colours."

Clo. Where, good Mistress Mary ?

---

28. *Nuncio*, Messenger.   31. *Diana.* See page 128.
34. *Semblative*, Like.   35. *Apt*, Fit for, favourable to.

Mar. In the wars ; and that may you be bold to say in your foolery.

Clo. Well, God give them wisdom that have it ; and those that are fools, let them use their talents.

Mar. Yet you will be hanged for being so long absent ; or to be turned away, is not that as good as a hanging to you ?

Clo. Many a good hanging prevents a bad marriage ; 20 and, for turning away, let summer bear it out.

Mar. You are resolute, then ?

Clo. Not so, neither ; but I am resolved on two points.

Mar. That if one break, the other will hold ; or, if both break, your gaskins fall.

Clo. Apt, in good faith ; very apt. Well, go thy way ; if Sir Toby would leave drinking, thou wert as witty a piece of Eve's flesh as any in Illyria.

Mar. Peace, you rogue, no more o' that. Here 30 comes my lady : make your excuse wisely, you were best.   [*Exit.*

Clo. Wit, an 't be thy will, put me into good fooling ! Those wits, that think they have thee, do very oft prove fools ; and I, that am sure I lack thee, may pass for a wise man : for what says Quinapalus ? " Better a witty fool than a foolish wit."

[*Enter* Lady Olivia *with* Malvolio.]

God bless thee, lady !

Oli. Take the fool away.

Clo. Do you not hear, fellows ? Take away the 40 lady.

Oli. Go to, you're a dry fool ; I'll no more of you : besides, you grow dishonest.

Clo. Two faults, madonna, that drink and good

23–25. *Points . . . gaskins.* The loose breeches, or *gaskins*, fashionable at the time, were fastened to the upper garment by tagged laces called *points.*
35. *Quinapalus*, an authority invented by Feste.
43. *Madonna*, My lady, Feste's individual way of addressing Olivia.

counsel will amend : for give the dry fool drink, then
is the fool not dry : bid the dishonest man mend himself ; if he mend, he is no longer dishonest ; if he
cannot, let the botcher mend him.   Anything that's
mended is but patched : virtue that transgresses is but
patched with sin ; and sin that amends is but patched
50 with virtue.   If that this simple syllogism will serve,
so ; if it will not, what remedy ?   The lady bade take
away the fool ; therefore, I say again, take her away.

Oli. Sir, I bade them take away you.

Clo. Misprision in the highest degree !   Lady, cucullus non facit monachum ; that's as much to say as I
wear not motley in my brain.   Good madonna, give
me leave to prove you a fool.

Oli. Can you do it ?

Clo. Dexterously, good madonna.

60 *Oli.* Make your proof.

Clo. I must catechize you for it, madonna : good my
mouse of virtue, answer me.

Oli. Well, sir, for want of other idleness, I'll bide
your proof.

Clo. Good madonna, why mournest thou ?

Oli. Good fool, for my brother's death.

Clo. I think his soul is in hell, madonna.

Oli. I know his soul is in heaven, fool.

Clo. The more fool, madonna, to mourn for your
70 brother's soul being in heaven.   Take away the fool,
gentlemen.

Oli. What think you of this fool, Malvolio ? doth he
not mend ?

Mal. Yes, and shall do till the pangs of death shake
him : infirmity, that decays the wise, doth ever make
the better fool.

47. *Botcher,* Patcher of old clothes or shoes.
50. *Syllogism,* Logical form of reasoning, deducing a conclusion from
       two given statements (*i.e.* All men are mortal.   Cæsar was
       a man.   Therefore Cæsar was mortal).
54. *Misprision,* Misunderstanding.
54-55. *Cucullus . . .* The cowl does not make the monk.

Clo. God send you, sir, a speedy infirmity, for the better increasing your folly! Sir Toby will be sworn that I am no fox; but he will not pass his word for 80 twopence that you are no fool.

Oli. How say you to that, Malvolio?

Mal. I marvel your ladyship takes delight in such a barren rascal: I saw him put down the other day with an ordinary fool that has no more brain than a stone. Look you now, he's out of his guard already; unless you laugh and minister occasion to him, he is gagged. I protest, I take these wise men, that crow so at these set kind of fools, no better than the fool's zanies.

Oli. O, you are sick of self-love, Malvolio, and taste 90 with a distempered appetite. To be generous, guiltless and of free disposition, is to take those things for bird-bolts that you deem cannon-bullets: there is no slander in an allowed fool, though he do nothing but rail; nor no railing in a known discreet man, though he do nothing but reprove.

Clo. Now Mercury endue thee with leasing, for thou speakest well of fools!

[Re-enter Maria.]

Mar. Madam, there is at the gate a young gentleman much desires to speak with you.

100 *Oli.* From the Count Orsino, is it?

Mar. I know not, madam: 'tis a fair young man, and well attended.

Oli. Who of my people hold him in delay?

Mar. Sir Toby, madam, your kinsman.

Oli. Fetch him off, I pray you; he speaks nothing but madman: fie on him! [*Exit* Maria.] Go you,

---

85. *Out of his guard*, Off his guard. The term is from fencing.
88. *Zanies.* The *zany* in Italian comedy imitates, in a clumsy way, the tricks and antics of the chief clown.
92. *Bird-bolts*, Short blunt-headed arrows that would kill small birds without piercing them. They would not do much harm to a human being.
96. *Mercury.* See page 128.   96. *Leasing*, Lying.

Malvolio ; if it be a suit from the count, I am sick, or
not at home ; what you will, to dismiss it. [*Exit*
MALVOLIO.] Now you see, sir, how your fooling grows
110 old, and people dislike it.

Clo. Thou hast spoke for us, madonna, as if thy
eldest son should be a fool ; whose skull Jove cram
with brains ! for,—here he comes,—one of thy kin has
a most weak pia mater.

[*Enter* SIR TOBY.]

Oli. By mine honour, half drunk. What is he at the
gate, cousin ?

Sir To. A gentleman.

Oli. A gentleman ! what gentleman ?

Sir To. 'Tis a gentleman here—a plague o' these
120 pickle-herring ! How now, sot !

Clo. Good Sir Toby !

Oli. Cousin, cousin, how have you come so early by
this lethargy ?

Sir To. Lethargy ! I defy lethargy. There's one at
the gate.

Oli. Ay, marry, what is he ?

Sir To. Let him be the devil, an he will, I care not :
give me faith, say I. Well, it's all one. [*Exit.*

Oli. What's a drunken man like, fool ?

130 *Clo.* Like a drowned man, a fool and a madman :
one draught above heat makes him a fool ; the second
mads him ; and a third drowns him.

Oli. Go thou and seek the crowner, and let him sit o'
my coz ; for he's in the third degree of drink, he's
drowned : go, look after him.

Clo. He is but mad yet, madonna ; and the fool
shall look to the madman. [*Exit.*

[*Re-enter* MALVOLIO.]

Mal. Madam, yond young fellow swears he will

---

114. *Pia mater*, The inner membrane covering the brain, here used
    of the brain itself.

speak with you. I told him you were sick ; he takes
140 on him to understand so much, and therefore comes to
speak with you. I told him you were asleep ; he
seems to have a foreknowledge of that too, and therefore comes to speak with you. What is to be said to
him, lady ? he's fortified against any denial.

Oli. Tell him he shall not speak with me.

Mal. Has been told so ; and he says, he'll stand at
your door like a sheriff's post, and be the supporter to
a bench, but he'll speak with you.

Oli. What kind o' man is he ?

150 *Mal.* Why, of mankind.

Oli. What manner of man ?

Mal. Of very ill manner ; he'll speak with you, will
you or no ?

Oli. Of what personage and years is he ?

Mal. Not yet old enough for a man, nor young
enough for a boy : as a squash is before 'tis a peascod,
or a codling when 'tis almost an apple ; 'tis with him
in standing water, between boy and man. He is very
well-favoured and he speaks very shrewishly ; one
160 would think his mother's milk were scarce out of him.

Oli. Let him approach : call in my gentlewoman.

Mal. Gentlewoman, my lady calls.   [*Exit.*

[*Re-enter* MARIA.]

Oli. Give me my veil : come, throw it o'er my face.
We'll once more hear Orsino's embassy.

[*Enter* VIOLA *and* Attendants.]

Vio. The honourable lady of the house, which is she ?

Oli. Speak to me ; I shall answer for her. Your
will ?

147. *Sheriff's post,* Fixed at the door of the sheriff for public notices,
    or simply to indicate his place of residence.
156. *Squash,* An unripe peascod.   157. *Codling,* An unripe apple.
158. *In standing water,* At the turn of the tide, neither one thing
    nor the other.   159. *Well-favoured,* Good-looking.
159. *Shrewishly,* Like a shrew, or sharp-tongued woman.

Vio. Most radiant, exquisite and unmatchable beauty,—I pray you, tell me if this be the lady of the house, for I never saw her: I would be loath to cast away my speech, for besides that it is excellently well penned, I have taken great pains to con it. Good beauties, let me sustain no scorn; I am very comptible, even to the least sinister usage.

Oli. Whence came you, sir?

Vio. I can say little more than I have studied, and that question's out of my part. Good gentle one, give me modest assurance if you be the lady of the house, that I may proceed in my speech.

Oli. Are you a comedian?

Vio. No, my profound heart: and yet, by the very fangs of malice I swear, I am not that I play. Are you the lady of the house?

Oli. If I do not usurp myself, I am.

Vio. Most certain, if you are she, you do usurp yourself; for what is yours to bestow is not yours to reserve. But this is from my commission: I will on with my speech in your praise, and then show you the heart of my message.

Oli. Come to what is important in 't: I forgive you the praise.

Vio. Alas, I took great pains to study it, and 'tis poetical.

Oli. It is the more like to be feigned: I pray you, keep it in. I heard you were saucy at my gates, and allowed your approach rather to wonder at you than to hear you. If you be not mad, be gone; if you have reason, be brief: 'tis not that time of moon with me to make one in so skipping a dialogue.

Mar. Will you hoist sail, sir? here lies your way.

Vio. No, good swabber; I am to hull here a little

---

173. *Comptible,* Sensitive.   174. *Sinister usage,* Unkind treatment.
198. *Time of moon.* The full moon was supposed to have a bad effect on an unbalanced mind.
199. *Skipping,* Frivolous.   201. *Hull,* Float.

longer.   Some mollification for your giant, sweet lady.
Tell me your mind : I am a messenger.

Oli. Sure, you have some hideous matter to deliver,
when the courtesy of it is so fearful.   Speak your
office.

Vio. It alone concerns your ear.   I bring no over-
ture of war, no taxation of homage : I hold the olive
in my hand ; my words are as full of peace as matter.

210   *Oli.* Yet you began rudely.   What are you ?   what
would you ?

Vio. The rudeness that hath appeared in me have
I learned from my entertainment.   What I am, and
what I would, are as secret as maidenhood ; to your
ears, divinity, to any other's, profanation.

Oli. Give us the place alone : we will hear this
divinity.   [*Exeunt* Maria *and Attendants.*]   Now, sir,
what is your text ?

Vio. Most sweet lady,—

220   *Oli.* A comfortable doctrine, and much may be said
of it.   Where lies your text ?

Vio. In Orsino's bosom.

Oli. In his bosom !   In what chapter of his bosom ?

Vio. To answer by the method, in the first of his
heart.

Oli. O, I have read it : it is heresy.   Have you no
more to say ?

Vio. Good madam, let me see your face.

Oli. Have you any commission from your lord to
230 negotiate with my face ?   You are now out of your
text : but we will draw the curtain and show you the
picture.   Look you, sir, such a one I was this present :
is 't not well done ?   [*Unveiling.*

Vio. Excellently done, if God did all.

Oli. 'Tis in grain, sir ; 'twill endure wind and
weather.

Vio. 'Tis beauty truly blent, whose red and white

208. *Taxation*, Claim.

Nature's own sweet and cunning hand laid on :
Lady, you are the cruell'st she alive,
240 If you will lead these graces to the grave
And leave the world no copy.

Oli. O, sir, I will not be so hard-hearted ; I will give
out divers schedules of my beauty : it shall be inven-
toried, and every particle and utensil labelled to my
will : as, item, two lips, indifferent red ; item, two
grey eyes, with lids to them ; item, one neck, one chin,
and so forth. Were you sent hither to praise me ?

Vio. I see what you are, you are too proud ;
But, if you were the devil, you are fair.
250 My lord and master loves you : O, such love
Could be but recompensed, though you were crown'd
The nonpareil of beauty !

Oli. How does he love me ?

Vio. With adorations, with fertile tears,
With groans that thunder love, with sighs of fire.

Oli. Your lord does know my mind ; I cannot love
     him :
Yet I suppose him virtuous, know him noble,
Of great estate, of fresh and stainless youth ;
In voices well divulged, free, learn'd and valiant ;
And in dimension and the shape of nature
260 A gracious person : but yet I cannot love him ;
He might have took his answer long ago.

Vio. If I did love you in my master's flame,
With such a suffering, such a deadly life,
In your denial I would find no sense ;
I would not understand it.

Oli. Why, what would you ?

Vio. Make me a willow cabin at your gate,
And call upon my soul within the house ;
Write loyal cantons of contemned love
And sing them loud even in the dead of night ;

---

252. *Nonpareil,* Unequalled one.
259. *Dimension,* Bodily proportion.
268. *Cantons,* Songs.

37

270 Halloo your name to the reverberate hills
And make the babbling gossip of the air
Cry out " Olivia ! "   O, you should not rest
Between the elements of air and earth,
But you should pity me !
 Oli.   You might do much.
What is your parentage ?
 Vio. Above my fortunes, yet my state is well :
I am a gentleman.
 Oli.   Get you to your lord ;
I cannot love him : let him send no more ;
Unless, perchance, you come to me again,
280 To tell me how he takes it.   Fare you well :
I thank you for your pains : spend this for me.
 Vio. I am no fee'd post, lady ; keep your purse :
My master, not myself, lacks recompense.
Love make his heart of flint that you shall love ;
And let your fervour, like my master's, be
Placed in contempt !   Farewell, fair cruelty.   [*Exit.*
 Oli. " What is your parentage ? "
" Above my fortunes, yet my state is well :
I am a gentleman."   I'll be sworn thou art ;
290 Thy tongue, thy face, thy limbs, actions and spirit,
Do give thee five-fold blazon : not too fast : soft, soft !
Unless the master were the man.   How now !
Even so quickly may one catch the plague ?
Methinks I feel this youth's perfections
With an invisible and subtle stealth
To creep in at mine eyes.   Well, let it be.
What ho, Malvolio !

[*Re-enter* MALVOLIO.]

 Mal.   Here, madam, at your service.
 Oli. Run after that same peevish messenger,

282. *Fee'd post,* Paid messenger.
291. *Blazon,* The description or the drawing of the coat-of-arms.
   Cesario's personal qualities proclaim or stamp him as a
   gentleman.

The county's man : he left this ring behind him,
300 Would I or not : tell him I'll none of it.
Desire him not to flatter with his lord,
Nor hold him up with hopes ; I'm not for him :
If that the youth will come this way to-morrow,
I'll give him reasons for 't : hie thee, Malvolio.

   Mal. Madam, I will.   ⌈*Exit.*

   Oli. I do I know not what, and fear to find
Mine eye too great a flatterer for my mind.
Fate, show thy force : ourselves we do not owe ;
What is decreed must be, and be this so.   ⌈*Exit*

   299. *County's,* Old form of count's.   308. *Owe,* Own.

ACT II

SCENE I

The sea-coast.

[*Enter* ANTONIO *and* SEBASTIAN.]

Ant. Will you stay no longer ? nor will you not that
I go with you ?

Seb. By your patience, no. My stars shine darkly
over me : the malignancy of my fate might perhaps
distemper yours ; therefore I shall crave of you your
leave that I may bear my evils alone : it were a bad
recompense for your love, to lay any of them on you.

Ant. Let me yet know of you whither you are bound.

Seb. No, sooth, sir : my determinate voyage is mere
10 extravagancy. But I perceive in you so excellent a
touch of modesty, that you will not extort from me
what I am willing to keep in ; therefore it charges me
in manners the rather to express myself. You must
know of me then, Antonio, my name is Sebastian,
which I called Roderigo. My father was that Sebastian of Messaline, whom I know you have heard of.
He left behind him myself and a sister, both born in an
hour : if the heavens had been pleased, would we had
so ended ! but you, sir, altered that ; for some hour
20 before you took me from the breach of the sea was my
sister drowned.

Ant. Alas the day !

Seb. A lady, sir, though it was said she much re-

---

4. *Malignancy,* Unfavourable aspect.   An astrological term.
5. *Distemper,* Disturb.   9. *Sooth,* Truth.
9. *Determinate,* Determined upon.   10. *Extravagancy,* Wandering.
13. *To express myself,* To say who I am.   20. *Breach,* Breaking.

sembled me, was yet of many accounted beautiful :
but, though I could not with such estimable wonder
overfar believe that, yet thus far I will boldly publish
her ; she bore a mind that envy could not but call fair.
She is drowned already, sir, with salt water, though I
seem to drown her remembrance again with more.

30 *Ant.* Pardon me, sir, your bad entertainment.

Seb. O good Antonio, forgive me your trouble.

Ant. If you will not murder me for my love, let me
be your servant.

Seb. If you will not undo what you have done, that
is, kill him whom you have recovered, desire it not.
Fare ye well at once : my bosom is full of kindness,
and I am yet so near the manners of my mother,
that upon the least occasion more mine eyes will tell
tales of me. I am bound to the Count Orsino's court :
40 farewell. [*Exit.*

Ant. The gentleness of all the gods go with thee !
I have many enemies in Orsino's court,
Else would I very shortly see thee there.
But, come what may, I do adore thee so,
That danger shall seem sport, and I will go. [*Exit.*

SCENE II

A street.

[*Enter* VIOLA, MALVOLIO *following.*]

Mal. Were you not even now with the Countess
Olivia ?

Vio. Even now, sir ; on a moderate pace I have
since arrived but hither.

Mal. She returns this ring to you, sir : you might

25. *Estimable wonder*, (*a*) Esteeming wonder (admiration), *i.e.*
    admiration and esteem, *estimable* being active in sense ; or
    (*b*) wonder (admiration) worthy of esteem. The general
    sense is that he, being so much like her, will not go quite so
    far as to believe in the beauty for which many have so much
    admiration. See page 144.

have saved me my pains, to have taken it away yourself. She adds, moreover, that you should put your
lord into a desperate assurance she will none of him :
and one thing more, that you be never so hardy to
10 come again in his affairs, unless it be to report your
lord's taking of this.   Receive it so.

Vio. She took the ring of me : I'll none of it.

Mal. Come, sir, you peevishly threw it to her ; and
her will is, it should be so returned : if it be worth
stooping for, there it lies in your eye ; if not, be it his
that finds it.   [*Exit.*

Vio. I left no ring with her : what means this lady ?
Fortune forbid my outside have not charm'd her !
She made good view of me ; indeed, so much,
20 That sure methought her eyes had lost her tongue,
For she did speak in starts distractedly.
She loves me, sure : the cunning of her passion
Invites me in this churlish messenger.
None of my lord's ring ! why, he sent her none.
I am the man : if it be so, as 't is,
Poor lady, she were better love a dream.
Disguise, I see, thou art a wickedness,
Wherein the pregnant enemy does much.
How easy is it for the proper-false
30 In women's waxen hearts to set their forms !
Alas, our frailty is the cause, not we !
For such as we are made of, such we be.
How will this fadge ? my master loves her dearly ;
And I, poor monster, fond as much on him ;
And she, mistaken, seems to dote on me.
What will become of this ?   As I am man,
My state is desperate for my master's love ;
As I am a woman,—now alas the day !—
What thriftless sighs shall poor Olivia breathe !
40 O time ! thou must untangle this, not I ;
It is too hard a knot for me to untie !   [*Exit.*

28. *Pregnant*, Ready-witted.   29. *Proper*, Handsome.
33. *Fadge*, Turn out.

SCENE III

A room in OLIVIA'S *house.*

[*Enter* SIR TOBY *and* SIR ANDREW.]

Sir To. Approach, Sir Andrew: not to be a-bed after midnight is to be up betimes ; and " diluculo surgere," thou know'st,—

Sir And. Nay, by my troth, I know not : but I know, to be up late is to be up late.

Sir To. A false conclusion : I hate it as an unfilled can. To be up after midnight and to go to bed then, is early : so that to go to bed after midnight is to go to bed betimes. Does not our life consist of the four 10 elements ?

Sir And. Faith, so they say ; but I think it rather consists of eating and drinking.

Sir To. Thou 'rt a scholar ; let us therefore eat and drink. Marian, I say ! a stoup of wine !

[*Enter* CLOWN.]

Sir And. Here comes the fool, i' faith.

Clo. How now, my hearts ! did you never see the picture of " we three " ?

2. *Betimes,* Early.
2. *Diluculo surgere saluberrimum est.* To rise early is most healthful, a phrase from Lily's Latin grammar, then in common use in schools.
9. *Four elements.* An old belief was that all existing things consist of these *elements,* earth, air, fire, and water, which, in the human body, appear as the *humours,* melancholy, blood, choler, and phlegm, on the proportion of which a man's health and disposition depended.
14. *Stoup,* Cup.
17. *We three.* Feste is thinking of a painted signboard, showing two fools, inscribed " We be three," thus drawing the reader into the company. On the stage he comes in behind Sir Toby and Sir Andrew, and thrusts his head, with its fool's cap, between them.

43

Sir To. Welcome, ass. Now let's have a catch.

Sir And. By my troth, the fool has an excellent
20 breast. I had rather than forty shillings I had such a
leg, and so sweet a breath to sing, as the fool has. In
sooth, thou wast in very gracious fooling last night,
when thou spokest of Pigrogromitus, of the Vapians
passing the equinoctial of Queubus : 'twas very
good, i' faith. I sent thee sixpence for thy leman :
hadst it ?

Clo. I did impeticos thy gratillity ; for Malvolio's
nose is no whipstock : my lady has a white hand, and
the Myrmidons are no bottle-ale houses.

30   *Sir And.* Excellent ! why, this is the best fooling,
when all is done. Now, a song.

Sir To. Come on ; there is sixpence for you : let's
have a song.

Sir And. There's a testril of me too : if one knight
give a—

Clo. Would you have a love-song, or a song of good
life ?

Sir To. A love-song, a love-song.

Sir And. Ay, ay : I care not for good life.

40   *Clo.* [*Sings*]

> O mistress mine, where are you roaming ?
> O, stay and hear ; your true love's coming,
>   That can sing both high and low :
> Trip no further, pretty sweeting ;
> Journeys end in lovers meeting,
>   Every wise man's son doth know.

Sir And. Excellent good, i' faith.

Sir To. Good, good.

Clo. [*Sings*]

> What is love ? 'tis not hereafter ;

18. *Catch,* Part-song, in which a number of singers sing the same
melody, the second beginning the first line as the first begins
the second, and so on.   20. *Breast,* Voice.
23. *Pigrogromitus, etc.* Here and in his next speech Feste gabbles
nonsense.   25. *Leman,* Sweetheart.   34. *Testril,* Sixpence.

50   Present mirth hath present laughter ;
        What's to come is still unsure :
    In delay there lies no plenty ;
        Then come kiss me, sweet and twenty,
        Youth's a stuff will not endure.

Sir And. A mellifluous voice, as I am true knight.

Sir To. A contagious breath.

Sir And. Very sweet and contagious, i' faith.

Sir To. To hear by the nose, it is dulcet in contagion.
But shall we make the welkin dance indeed ? shall we
60 rouse the night-owl in a catch that will draw three
souls out of one weaver ? shall we do that ?

Sir And. An you love me, let's do 't : I am dog at
a catch.

Clo. By 'r lady, sir, and some dogs will catch
well.

Sir And. Most certain. Let our catch be, " Thou
knave."

Clo. " Hold thy peace, thou knave," knight ? I
shall be constrained in 't to call thee knave, knight.

70 *Sir And.* 'Tis not the first time I have constrained
one to call me knave. Begin, fool : it begins " Hold
thy peace."

Clo. I shall never begin if I hold my peace.

Sir And. Good, i' faith. Come, begin. [*Catch sung.*

[*Enter* MARIA.]

Mar. What a caterwauling do you keep here ! If
my lady have not called up her steward Malvolio and
bid him turn you out of doors, never trust me.

Sir To. My lady's a Cataian, we are politicians,
Malvolio's a Peg-a-Ramsey, and " Three merry men

60. *Welkin*, Sky.
61–62. *Catch . . . weaver.* Many of the Elizabethan weavers were
      Calvinistic refugees who had fled from persecution in the
      Netherlands. A catch that could have the effect here de-
      scribed would be a wonderful catch indeed.
78. *Cataian*, Native of Cathay, or China, a term of reproach.
79. *Peg-a-Ramsey*, the name of an old ballad. See page 122.

80 be we."   Am not I consanguineous ? am I not of her
blood ? Tillyvally. Lady ! [*Sings*] " There dwelt a
man in Babylon, lady, lady ! "

Clo. Beshrew me, the knight's in admirable fooling.

Sir And. Ay, he does well enough if he be disposed,
and so do I too : he does it with a better grace, but I
do it more natural.

Sir To. [*Sings*] " O, the twelfth day of December,"—

Mar. For the love o' God, peace !

[*Enter* Malvolio.]

Mal. My masters, are you mad ? or what are you ?
90 Have you no wit, manners, nor honesty, but to gabble
like tinkers at this time of night ?   Do ye make
an alehouse of my lady's house, that ye squeak out
your coziers' catches without any mitigation or re-
morse of voice ?   Is there no respect of place, persons,
nor time in you ?

Sir To. We did keep time, sir, in our catches.
Sneck up !

Mal. Sir Toby, I must be round with you.   My lady
bade me tell you, that, though she harbours you as her
100 kinsman, she's nothing allied to your disorders.   If
you can separate yourself and your misdemeanours,
you are welcome to the house ; if not, an it would
please you to take leave of her, she is very willing to
bid you farewell.

Sir To. " Farewell, dear heart, since I must needs
be gone."

Mar. Nay, good Sir Toby.

Clo. " His eyes do show his days are almost done."

Mal. Is 't even so ?

110 *Sir To.* " But I will never die."

Clo. Sir Toby, there you lie.

81. *Tillyvally*, an expression of contempt.
83. *Beshrew me*, May evil come to me—used as a mere exclamation.
93. *Coziers*, Cobblers.   97. *Sneck up !* Go and be hanged !
98. *Round*, Plain-spoken.

46

Mal. This is much credit to you.

Sir To. "Shall I bid him go?"

Clo. "What an if you do?"

Sir To. "Shall I bid him go, and spare not?"

Clo. "O no, no, no, no, you dare not."

Sir To. Out o' tune, sir: ye lie. Art any more than a steward? Dost thou think, because thou art virtuous, there shall be no more cakes and ale?

120 *Clo.* Yes, by Saint Anne, and ginger shall be hot i' the mouth too.

Sir To. Thou'rt i' the right. Go, sir, rub your chain with crumbs. A stoup of wine, Maria!

Mal. Mistress Mary, if you prized my lady's favour at any thing more than contempt, you would not give means for this uncivil rule: she shall know of it, by this hand.   [*Exit.*

Mar. Go shake your ears.

Sir And. 'Twere as good a deed as to drink when a
130 man's a-hungry, to challenge him the field, and then to break promise with him and make a fool of him.

Sir To. Do 't, knight: I'll write thee a challenge; or I'll deliver thy indignation to him by word of mouth.

Mar. Sweet Sir Toby, be patient for to-night: since the youth of the count's was to-day with my lady, she is much out of quiet. For Monsieur Malvolio, let me alone with him: if I do not gull him into a nayword, and make him a common recreation, do
140 not think I have wit enough to lie straight in my bed: I know I can do it.

Sir To. Possess us, possess us; tell us something of him.

Mar. Marry, sir, sometimes he is a kind of puritan.

---

119. *Cakes and ale,* representing the good material things of life.
120. *Ginger,* used for flavouring ale.
122. *Rub . . . crumbs.* The chain Malvolio wears as a badge of office would be cleaned in this way.
139. *Nayword,* Byword.   139. *Recreation,* Laughing-stock.
142. *Possess us,* Tell us.

Sir And. O, if I thought that, I 'ld beat him like a dog !

Sir To. What, for being a puritan ! thy exquisite reason, dear knight ?

Sir And. I have no exquisite reason for 't, but I
150 have reason good enough.

Mar. The devil a puritan that he is, or any thing constantly, but a time-pleaser ; an affectioned ass, that cons state without book and utters it by great swarths : the best persuaded of himself, so crammed, as he thinks, with excellencies, that it is his grounds of faith that all that look on him love him ; and on that vice in him will my revenge find notable cause to work.

Sir To. What wilt thou do ?

160 *Mar.* I will drop in his way some obscure epistles of love ; wherein, by the colour of his beard, the shape of his leg, the manner of his gait, the expressure of his eye, forehead, and complexion, he shall find himself most feelingly personated. I can write very like my lady your niece : on a forgotten matter we can hardly make distinction of our hands.

Sir To. Excellent ! I smell a device.

Sir And. I have 't in my nose too.

Sir To. He shall think, by the letters that thou wilt
170 drop, that they come from my niece, and that she's in love with him.

Mar. My purpose is, indeed, a horse of that colour.

Sir And. And your horse now would make him an ass.

Mar. Ass, I doubt not.

Sir And. O, 'twill be admirable !

Mar. Sport royal, I warrant you : I know my physic will work with him. I will plant you two, and let

152. *Affectioned,* Affected.
153. *Cons state without book,* Learns up " arguments of state " by heart. " Without book " is an actor's phrase.
154. *Swarths,* Swathes of grass. Consider the appropriateness of the metaphor.

48

the fool make a third, where he shall find the letter:
180 observe his construction of it.   For this night, to bed,
and dream on the event.   Farewell.   [*Exit.*

Sir To. Good night, Penthesilea.

Sir And. Before me, she's a good wench.

Sir To. She's a beagle, true-bred, and one that adores
me : what o' that ?

Sir And. I was adored once too.

Sir To. Let's to bed, knight.   Thou hadst need send
for more money.

Sir And. If I cannot recover your niece, I am a foul
190 way out.

Sir To. Send for money, knight : if thou hast her
not i' the end, call me cut.

Sir And. If I do not, never trust me, take it how
you will.

Sir To. Come, come, I'll go burn some sack ; 'tis
too late to go to bed now : come, knight ; come,
knight.   [*Exeunt.*

SCENE IV

A room in the DUKE'S *palace.*

[*Enter* DUKE, VIOLA, CURIO, *and others.*]

Duke. Give me some music.   Now, good morrow,
      friends.
Now, good Cesario, but that piece of song,
That old and antique song we heard last night :
Methought it did relieve my passion much,
More than light airs and recollected terms

---

192. *Cut,* A bob-tailed horse.   The old slang phrase " Call me cut,"
      means " Call me a fool."
195. *Sack,* Light dry Spanish wine.   *Burnt sack* was mulled, *i.e.*
      warmed, sweetened, and spiced.
5. *Recollected terms,* Words which are the result of memory and
      choice, contrasted with the spontaneous phrasing of the
      language of the song Orsino likes.

Of these most brisk and giddy-paced times :
Come, but one verse.

    Cur. He is not here, so please your lordship, that
should sing it.

10   *Duke.* Who was it ?

    Cur. Feste, the jester, my lord ; a fool that the lady
Olivia's father took much delight in. He is about
the house.

    Duke. Seek him out, and play the tune the while.

                        [*Exit* Curio. *Music plays.*

Come hither, boy : if ever thou shalt love,
In the sweet pangs of it remember me ;
For such as I am all true lovers are,
Unstaid and skittish in all motions else,
Save in the constant image of the creature

20 That is beloved. How dost thou like this tune ?

    Vio. It gives a very echo to the seat
Where Love is throned.

    Duke. Thou dost speak masterly :
My life upon 't, young though thou art, thine eye
Hath stay'd upon some favour that it loves :
Hath it not, boy ?

    Vio.   A little, by your favour.

    Duke. What kind of woman is 't ?

    Vio.   Of your complexion.

    Duke. She is not worth thee, then. What years, i'
    faith ?

    Vio. About your years, my lord.

30   *Duke.* Too old, by heaven : let still the woman take
An elder than herself ; so wears she to him,
So sways she level in her husband's heart :
For, boy, however we do praise ourselves,
Our fancies are more giddy and unfirm,
More longing, wavering, sooner lost and worn,
Than women's are.

    Vio   I think it well, my lord.

---

18. *Motions*, Emotions.   25. *Favour*, Face.
27. *Complexion*, General appearance or temperament.

Duke. Then let thy love be younger than thyself,
Or thy affection cannot hold the bent ;
For women are as roses, whose fair flower
40 Being once display'd, doth fall that very hour.
　　Vio. And so they are : alas, that they are so ;
To die, even when they to perfection grow !

[*Re-enter* CURIO *and* CLOWN.]

Duke. O, fellow, come, the song we had last night.
Mark it, Cesario, it is old and plain ;
The spinsters and the knitters in the sun
And the free maids that weave their thread with bones
Do use to chant it : it is silly sooth,
And dallies with the innocence of love,
Like the old age.
50　　*Clo.* Are you ready, sir ?
　　Duke. Ay ; prithee, sing. 　　　　　[*Music.*

[SONG.]

　　Clo. Come away, come away, death,
　　　　　And in sad cypress let me be laid ;
　　Fly away, fly away, breath ;
　　　　　I am slain by a fair cruel maid.
　　My shroud of white, stuck all with yew,
　　　　　O, prepare it !
　　My part of death, no one so true
　　　　　Did share it.

60　　　　Not a flower, not a flower sweet,
　　　　　On my black coffin let there be strown ;
　　Not a friend, not a friend greet
　　　　　My poor corpse, where my bones shall
　　　　　be thrown :

---

38. *Hold the bent,* Stand the strain, endure. The metaphor is from
　　the tension of the bow-string when stretched.
45. *Spinsters,* Feminine of spinners. 　**46.** *Free,* Free from care.
46. *Bones,* Bobbins made of bone. 　**47.** *Do use,* Are accustomed.
47. *Silly sooth,* Simple truth.

A thousand thousand sighs to save,
  Lay me, O, where
Sad true lover never find my grave,
  To weep there !

Duke. There's for thy pains.

Clo. No pains, sir ; I take pleasure in singing, sir.

70 *Duke.* I'll pay thy pleasure then.

Clo. Truly, sir, and pleasure will be paid, one time or another.

Duke. Give me now leave to leave thee.

Clo. Now, the melancholy god protect thee ; and the tailor make thy doublet of changeable taffeta, for thy mind is a very opal. I would have men of such constancy put to sea, that their business might be every thing and their intent every where ; for that's it that always makes a good voyage of nothing.
80 Farewell.   [*Exit.*

Duke. Let all the rest give place.
      [Curio *and Attendants retire.*
        Once more, Cesario,
Get thee to yond same sovereign cruelty :
Tell her, my love, more noble than the world,
Prizes not quantity of dirty lands ;
The parts that fortune hath bestow'd upon her,
Tell her, I hold as giddily as fortune ;
But 'tis that miracle and queen of gems
That nature pranks her in attracts my soul.

Vio. But if she cannot love you, sir ?

90 *Duke.* I cannot be so answer'd.

Vio.   Sooth, but you must.
Say that some lady, as perhaps there is,
Hath for your love as great a pang of heart
As you have for Olivia : you cannot love her ;
You tell her so ; must she not then be answer'd ?

Duke. There is no woman's sides

---

75. *Changeable*, Shot. 85. *Parts*, Gifts of rank, money, etc.
  86. *Hold*, Regard.   88. *Pranks*, Adorns.

Can bide the beating of so strong a passion
As love doth give my heart ; no woman's heart
So big, to hold so much ; they lack retention.
Alas, their love may be call'd appetite,
100 No motion of the liver, but the palate,
That suffer surfeit, cloyment and revolt :
But mine is all as hungry as the sea,
And can digest as much : make no compare
Between that love a woman can bear me
And that I owe Olivia.
    Vio.   Ay, but I know—
    Duke. What dost thou know ?
    Vio. Too well what love women to men may owe:
In faith, they are as true of heart as we.
My father had a daughter loved a man,
110 As it might be, perhaps, were I a woman,
I should your lordship.
    Duke.   And what's her history ?
    Vio. A blank, my lord. She never told her love,
But let concealment, like a worm i' the bud,
Feed on her damask cheek : she pined in thought,
And with a green and yellow melancholy
She sat like patience on a monument,
Smiling at grief. Was not this love indeed ?
We men may say more, swear more : but indeed
Our shows are more than will ; for still we prove
120 Much in our vows, but little in our love.
    Duke. But died thy sister of her love, my boy ?
    Vio. I am all the daughters of my father's house,
And all the brothers too : and yet I know not.
Sir, shall I to this lady ?
    Duke.   Ay, that's the theme.
To her in haste ; give her this jewel ; say,
My love can give no place, bide no denay. [*Exeunt.*

100. *Liver*, supposed to be the seat of the passions, especially love.
107. *Owe*, Possess.
114. *Damask*, like the damask rose (red, or red and white).
126. *Give place*, Withdraw.   126. *Denay*, Denial.

SCENE V

OLIVIA'S *garden.*

[*Enter* SIR TOBY, SIR ANDREW, *and* FABIAN.]

Sir To. Come thy ways, Signior Fabian.

Fab. Nay, I'll come : if I lose a scruple of this sport, let me be boiled to death with melancholy.

Sir To. Wouldst thou not be glad to have the niggardly rascally sheep-biter come by some notable shame ?

Fab. I would exult, man : you know, he brought me out o' favour with my lady about a bear-baiting here.

Sir To. To anger him we'll have the bear again ; and we will fool him black and blue : shall we not, Sir Andrew ?

Sir And. An we do not, it is pity of our lives.

Sir To. Here comes the little villain.

[*Enter* MARIA.]

How now, my metal of India !

Mar. Get ye all three into the box-tree : Malvolio's coming down this walk : he has been yonder i' the sun practising behaviour to his own shadow this half hour : observe him, for the love of mockery ; for I know this letter will make a contemplative idiot of him. Close, in the name of jesting ! Lie thou there [*throws down a letter*] ; for here comes the trout that must be caught with tickling.   [*Exit.*

[*Enter* MALVOLIO.]

Mal. 'Tis but a fortune ; all is fortune. Maria once told me she did affect me : and I have heard herself

---

5. *Sheep-biter,* A dog that worries sheep, hence a term of abuse.
20. *Close,* Keep hidden.   24. *Affect me,* Like me.

come thus near, that, should she fancy, it should be one of my complexion. Besides, she uses me with a more exalted respect than any one else that follows her. What should I think on't?

Sir To. Here's an overweening rogue!

30 *Fab.* O, peace! Contemplation makes a rare turkey-cock of him: how he jets under his advanced plumes!

Sir And. 'S light, I could so beat the rogue!

Sir To. Peace, I say.

Mal. To be Count Malvolio!

Sir To. Ah, rogue!

Sir And. Pistol him, pistol him.

Sir To. Peace, peace!

Mal. There is example for't; the lady of the Strachy married the yeoman of the wardrobe.

40 *Sir And.* Fie on him, Jezebel!

Fab. O, peace! now he's deeply in: look how imagination blows him.

Mal. Having been three months married to her, sitting in my state,—

Sir To. O, for a stone-bow, to hit him in the eye!

Mal. Calling my officers about me, in my branched velvet gown; having come from a day-bed, where I have left Olivia sleeping,—

Sir To. Fire and brimstone!

50 *Fab.* O, peace, peace!

Mal. And then to have the humour of state; and after a demure travel of regard, telling them I know my place as I would they should do theirs, to ask for kinsman Toby,—

Sir To. Bolts and shackles!

Fab. O peace, peace, peace! now, now.

Mal. Seven of my people, with an obedient start,

---

31. *Jets*, Struts.   31. *Advanced*, Puffed up.
38. *Lady of the Strachy.* The exact allusion is unknown, but the story of the love of the highborn lady for the squire of low degree is fairly common in ballad and romance.
39. *Yeoman*, Servant.   44. *State*, Chair of state.
45. *Stone-bow*, A cross-bow for shooting stones.

make out for him : I frown the while ; and perchance
wind up my watch, or play with my—some rich jewel.
60 Toby approaches ; courtesies there to me,—

Sir To. Shall this fellow live ?

Fab. Though our silence be drawn from us with
cars, yet peace.

Mal. I extend my hand to him thus, quenching my
familiar smile with an austere regard of control,—

Sir To. And does not Toby take you a blow o' the
lips then ?

Mal. Saying, " Cousin Toby, my fortunes having
cast me on your niece give me this prerogative of
70 speech,"—

Sir To. What, what ?

Mal. " You must amend your drunkenness."

Sir To. Out, scab !

Fab. Nay, patience, or we break the sinews of our
plot.

Mal. " Besides, you waste the treasure of your time
with a foolish knight,"—

Sir And. That's me, I warrant you.

Mal. " One Sir Andrew,"—

80   *Sir And.* I knew 'twas I ; for many do call me fool.

Mal. What employment have we here ?

[*Taking up the letter.*

Fab. Now is the woodcock near the gin.

Sir To. O, peace ! and the spirit of humours intimate reading aloud to him !

Mal. By my life, this is my lady's hand : these be
her very C's, her U's and her T's ; and thus makes she
her great P's. It is, in contempt of question, her
hand.

Sir And. Her C's, her U's and her T's ; why that ?

90   *Mal.* [*Reads*] " To the unknown beloved, this, and

---

63. *Cars.* He is thinking of the horrible punishment practised in
      ancient Rome, by which a man was torn asunder by being
      bound to chariots which were driven in opposite directions.
82. *Gin*, Snare.   84. *Intimate*, Suggest.

my good wishes:"—her very phrases! By your
leave, wax. Soft! and the impressure her Lucrece,
with which she uses to seal: 'tis my lady. To whom
should this be?

Fab. This wins him, liver and all.

Mal. [*Reads*]

> Jove knows I love:
>   But who?
> Lips, do not move;
> No man must know.

100 " No man must know." What follows? the numbers
altered! " No man must know:" if this should be
thee, Malvolio?

Sir To. Marry, hang thee, brock!

Mal. [*Reads*]

> I may command where I adore;
>   But silence, like a Lucrece knife,
> With bloodless stroke my heart doth gore:
>   M, O, A, I, doth sway my life.

Fab. A fustian riddle!

Sir To. Excellent wench, say I.

110 *Mal.* " M, O, A, I, doth sway my life." Nay, but
first, let me see, let me see, let me see.

Fab. What dish o' poison has she dressed him!

Sir To. And with what wing the staniel checks at it!

Mal. " I may command where I adore." Why, she
may command me: I serve her; she is my lady.
Why, this is evident to any formal capacity; there
is no obstruction in this: and the end,—what should
that alphabetical position portend? If I could make
that resemble something in me,—Softly! M, O, A, I,—

92. *Impressure,* Impression of the seal. A common device for
   ladies' seals represented the Roman matron Lucretia, who
   ended her life by stabbing herself. This explains " Lucrece
   knife " in Maria's verses.
103. *Brock,* Badger.   113. *Staniel,* A kind of falcon.
113. *Checks.* The falcon is said to check when it forsakes the prey
   at which it is flown for another.
116. *Formal capacity,* Rational intelligence.

120 *Sir To.* O, ay, make up that: he is now at a cold scent.

Fab. Sowter will cry upon't for all this, though it be as rank as a fox.

Mal. M,—Malvolio; M,—why, that begins my name.

Fab. Did not I say he would work it out? the cur is excellent at faults.

Mal. M,—but then there is no consonancy in the sequel; that suffers under probation: A should 130 follow, but O does.

Fab. And O shall end, I hope.

Sir To. Ay, or I'll cudgel him, and make him cry O!

Mal. And then I comes behind.

Fab. Ay, an you had any eye behind you, you might see more detraction at your heels than fortunes before you.

Mal. M, O, A, I; this simulation is not as the former: and yet, to crush this a little, it would bow to me, for every one of these letters are in my name. 140 Soft! here follows prose. [*Reads*] "If this fall into thy hand, revolve. In my stars I am above thee; but be not afraid of greatness: some are born great, some achieve greatness, and some have greatness thrust upon 'em. Thy Fates open their hands: let thy blood and spirit embrace them; and, to inure thyself to what thou art like to be, cast thy humble slough and appear fresh. Be opposite with a kinsman, surly with servants; let thy tongue tang arguments of state; put thyself into the trick of 150 singularity: she thus advises thee that sighs for thee.

122–127. *Sowter . . . cry upon . . . faults*, Name of a hound . . . give tongue, as a hound finding scent . . . wrong trails. Sir Toby says that Malvolio is at a *cold* scent (one hard to find); to Fabian the point is that you can trust him to work out the *wrong* scent, though it be "rank as a fox," for which no first-rate hound would forsake the scent of the hare.

128. *Consonancy*, Agreement.

137. *Simulation*, Disguise.   147. *Slough*, The snake's cast-off skin.

147. *Opposite*, Contradictory.   150. *Singularity*, Affectation.

Remember who commended thy yellow stockings, and wished to see thee ever cross-gartered : I say, remember. Go to, thou art made, if thou desirest to be so ; if not, let me see thee a steward still, the fellow of servants, and not worthy to touch Fortune's fingers. Farewell. She that would alter services with thee,   THE FORTUNATE UNHAPPY."

Daylight and champain discovers not more : this is open. I will be proud, I will read politic authors, I
160 will baffle Sir Toby, I will wash off gross acquaintance, I will be point-devise the very man. I do not now fool myself, to let imagination jade me ; for every reason excites to this, that my lady loves me. She did commend my yellow stockings of late, she did praise my leg being cross-gartered ; and in this she manifests herself to my love, and with a kind of injunction drives me to these habits of her liking. I thank my stars I am happy. I will be strange, stout, in yellow stockings, and cross-gartered, even with
170 the swiftness of putting on. Jove and my stars be praised ! Here is yet a postscript.

[*Reads*] " Thou canst not choose but know who I am. If thou entertainest my love, let it appear in thy smiling ; thy smiles become thee well ; therefore in my presence still smile, dear my sweet, I prithee."

Jove, I thank thee : I will smile ; I will do everything that thou wilt have me.   [*Exit*.

Fab. I will not give my part of this sport for a pension of thousands to be paid from the Sophy.

180   *Sir To.* I could marry this wench for this device.

Sir And. So could I too.

Sir To. And ask no other dowry with her but such another jest.

Sir And. Nor I neither.

Fab. Here comes my noble gull-catcher.

158. *Champain,* Open country.   161. *Point-devise,* Exactly.
168. *Strange,* Stand-offish.   168. *Stout,* Haughty.
179. *Sophy,* The Shah of Persia.

[Re-enter Maria.]

Sir To. Wilt thou set thy foot o' my neck ?

Sir And. Or o' mine either ?

Sir To. Shall I play my freedom at tray-trip, and become thy bond-slave ?

190   *Sir And.* I' faith, or I either ?

Sir To. Why, thou hast put him in such a dream, that when the image of it leaves him he must run mad.

Mar. If you will then see the fruits of the sport, mark his first approach before my lady : he will come to her in yellow stockings, and 'tis a colour she abhors, and cross-gartered, a fashion she detests ; and he will smile upon her, which will now be so unsuitable to her disposition, being addicted to a melancholy as she is, that it cannot but turn him into a notable contempt.
200 If you will see it, follow me.

Sir To. To the gates of Tartar, thou most excellent devil of wit !

Sir And. I'll make one too.   [*Exeunt.*

188. *Tray-trip*, a game at dice in which the lucky throw is a *trey*, or three.

ACT III

SCENE I

OLIVIA'S *garden.*

[*Enter* VIOLA, *and* CLOWN *with a tabor.*]

Vio. Save thee, friend, and thy music : dost thou
live by thy tabor ?

Clo. No, sir, I live by the church.

Vio. Art thou a churchman ?

Clo. No such matter, sir : I do live by the church ;
for I do live at my house, and my house doth stand
by the church.

Vio. So thou mayst say, the king lies by a beggar,
if a beggar dwells near him ; or, the church stands by
10 thy tabor, if thy tabor stand by the church.

Clo. You have said, sir. To see this age ! A sentence is but a cheveril glove to a good wit : how
quickly the wrong side may be turned outward !

Vio. Nay, that's certain ; they that dally nicely
with words may quickly make them wanton.

Clo. Indeed words are very rascals since bonds disgraced them.

Vio. Thy reason, man ?

Clo. Troth, sir, I can yield you none without words ;

10. *Tabor*, A small drum.   12. *Cheveril*, Soft leather.
14. *Dally nicely with words*, Play subtly with the meanings of words,
    as the Elizabethans loved to do.
16. *Bonds*. See page 125.

20 and words are grown so false, I am loath to prove
reason with them.

Vio. I warrant thou art a merry fellow and carest
for nothing.

Clo. Not so, sir, I do care for something; but in
my conscience, sir, I do not care for you: if that be
to care for nothing, sir, I would it would make you
invisible.

Vio. Art not thou the Lady Olivia's fool?

Clo. No, indeed, sir; the Lady Olivia has no folly:
30 she will keep no fool, sir, till she be married; and
fools are as like husbands as pilchards are to herrings;
the husband's the bigger: I am indeed not her fool,
but her corrupter of words.

Vio. I saw thee late at the Count Orsino's.

Clo. Foolery, sir, does walk about the orb like the
sun, it shines everywhere. I would be sorry, sir, but
the fool should be as oft with your master as with my
mistress: I think I saw your wisdom there.

Vio. Nay, an thou pass upon me, I'll no more with
40 thee. Hold, there's expenses for thee.

Clo. Now Jove, in his next commodity of hair, send
thee a beard!

Vio. By my troth, I'll tell thee, I am almost sick
for one; [*Aside*] though I would not have it grow on
my chin. Is thy lady within?

Clo. My lady is within, sir. I will construe to them
whence you come; who you are and what you would
are out of my welkin, I might say " element," but
the word is over-worn.   [*Exit.*

50   *Vio.* This fellow is wise enough to play the fool;
And to do that well craves a kind of wit:
He must observe their mood on whom he jests,
The quality of persons, and the time,
And, like the haggard, check at every feather
That comes before his eye. This is a practice

41. *Commodity*, Cargo.   53. *Quality*, Rank.
54. *Haggard*, An untrained hawk.

As full of labour as a wise man's art :
For folly that he wisely shows is fit ;
But wise men, folly-fall'n, quite taint their wit.

[*Enter* SIR TOBY *and* SIR ANDREW.]

    Sir To. Save you, gentleman.
60   *Vio.* And you, sir.
    Sir And. Dieu vous garde, monsieur.
    Vio. Et vous aussi ; votre serviteur.
    Sir And. I hope, sir, you are ; and I am yours.
    Sir To. Will you encounter the house ? my niece is desirous you should enter, if your trade be to her.
    Vio. I am bound to your niece, sir ; I mean, she is the list of my voyage.
    Sir To. Taste your legs, sir ; put them to motion.
    Vio. My legs do better understand me, sir, than I
70 understand what you mean by bidding me taste my legs.
    Sir To. I mean, to go, sir, to enter.
    Vio. I will answer you with gait and entrance. But we are prevented.

[*Enter* OLIVIA *and* MARIA.]

Most excellent accomplished lady, the heavens rain odours on you !
    Sir And. That youth's a rare courtier : " Rain odours ; " well.
    Vio. My matter hath no voice, lady, but to your
80 own most pregnant and vouchsafed ear.
    Sir And. " Odours," " pregnant," and " vouchsafed " : I'll get 'em all three all ready.
    Oli. Let the garden door be shut, and leave me to my hearing. [*Exeunt* SIR TOBY, SIR ANDREW, *and* MARIA.] Give me your hand, sir.

67. *List,* Limit.
68. *Taste,* Make trial of. The first part of this scene is full of
    laughing mockery of contemporary affectation in talk.
74. *Prevented,* Forestalled.

Vio. My duty, madam, and most humble service.

Oli. What is your name?

Vio. Cesario is your servant's name, fair princess.

Oli. My servant, sir! 'Twas never merry world
90 Since lowly feigning was called compliment:
You're servant to the Count Orsino, youth.

Vio. And he is yours, and his must needs be yours:
Your servant's servant is your servant, madam.

Oli. For him, I think not on him: for his thoughts
Would they were blanks, rather than fill'd with me!

Vio. Madam, I come to whet your gentle thoughts
On his behalf.

Oli.   O, by your leave, I pray you,
I bade you never speak again of him:
But, would you undertake another suit,
100 I had rather hear you to solicit that
Than music from the spheres.

Vio.   Dear lady,—

Oli. Give me leave, beseech you. I did send,
After the last enchantment you did here,
A ring in chase of you: so did I abuse
Myself, my servant and, I fear me, you:
Under your hard construction must I sit,
To force that on you, in a shameful cunning,
Which you knew none of yours: what might you
     think?
Have you not set mine honour at the stake
110 And baited it with all the unmuzzled thoughts
That tyrannous heart can think? To one of your re-
     ceiving
Enough is shown: a cypress, not a bosom,
Hideth my heart. So, let me hear you speak.

Vio. I pity you.

---

101. *Music from the spheres.* According to the old system of as-
     tronomy, called the *Ptolemaic* system, after the astronomer
     Ptolemy, the revolving spheres containing the sun, moon,
     and the planets made this marvellous music as they moved
     round the earth.
111. *Receiving,* Capacity for understanding.

64

Oli.   That's a degree to love.

Vio. No, not a grize ; for 'tis a vulgar proof,
That very oft we pity enemies.

Oli. Why, then, methinks 'tis time to smile again.
O world, how apt the poor are to be proud !
If one should be a prey, how much the better
120 To fall before the lion than the wolf !   [*Clock strikes.*
The clock upbraids me with the waste of time.
Be not afraid, good youth, I will not have you :
And yet, when wit and youth is come to harvest,
Your wife is like to reap a proper man :
There lies your way, due west.

Vio. Then westward-ho !   Grace and good disposi-
tion
Attend your ladyship !
You'll nothing, madam, to my lord by me ?

Oli. Stay :
130 I prithee, tell me what thou think'st of me.

Vio. That you do think you are not what you are.

Oli. If I think so, I think the same of you.

Vio. Then think you right : I am not what I am.

Oli. I would you were as I would have you be !

Vio. Would it be better, madam, than I am ?
I wish it might, for now I am your fool.

Oli. O, what a deal of scorn looks beautiful
In the contempt and anger of his lip !
A murderous guilt shows not itself more soon
140 Than love that would seem hid : love's night is noon.
Cesario, by the roses of the spring,
By maidhood, honour, truth and everything,
I love thee so, that, maugre all thy pride,
Nor wit nor reason can my passion hide.
Do not extort thy reasons from this clause,
For that I woo, thou therefore hast no cause ;
But rather reason thus with reason fetter,
Love sought is good, but given unsought is better.

115. *Grize*, Step.   115. *Vulgar proof*, Common experience.
143. *Maugre*, In spite of.

Vio. By innocence I swear, and by my youth,
150 I have one heart, one bosom and one truth,
And that no woman has ; nor never none
Shall mistress be of it, save I alone.
And so adieu, good madam : nevermore
Will I my master's tears to you deplore.
   Oli. Yet come again ; for thou perhaps mayst move
That heart, which now abhors, to like his love.

                             [Exeunt.

SCENE II

A room in Olivia's *house.*

[*Enter* Sir Toby, Sir Andrew, *and* Fabian.]

   Sir And. No, faith, I'll not stay a jot longer.
   Sir To. Thy reason, dear venom, give thy reason.
   Fab. You must needs yield your reason, Sir Andrew.
   Sir And. Marry, I saw your niece do more favours
to the count's serving-man than ever she bestowed
upon me ; I saw't i' the orchard.
   Sir To. Did she see thee the while, old boy? tell
me that.
   Sir And. As plain as I see you now.
10   *Fab.* This was a great argument of love in her
toward you.
   Sir And. 'S light, will you make an ass o' me ?
   Fab. I will prove it legitimate, sir, upon the oaths
of judgment and reason.
   Sir To. And they have been grand-jurymen since
before Noah was a sailor.
   Fab. She did show favour to the youth in your sight
only to exasperate you, to awake your dormouse
valour, to put fire in your heart, and brimstone in your
20 liver. You should then have accosted her ; and with

6. *Orchard*, Garden.   10. *Argument*, Proof.

some excellent jests, fire-new from the mint, you
should have banged the youth into dumbness. This
was looked for at your hand, and this was balked:
the double gilt of this opportunity you let time wash
off, and you are now sailed into the north of my lady's
opinion ; where you will hang like an icicle on a
Dutchman's beard, unless you do redeem it by some
laudable attempt either of valour or policy.

   Sir And. An't be any way, it must be with valour ;
30 for policy I hate : I had as lief be a Brownist as a
politician.

   Sir To. Why, then, build me thy fortunes upon the
basis of valour. Challenge me the count's youth to
fight with him ; hurt him in eleven places : my niece
shall take note of it ; and assure thyself, there is no
love-broker in the world can more prevail in man's
commendation with woman than report of valour.

   Fab. There is no way but this, Sir Andrew.

   Sir And. Will either of you bear me a challenge
40 to him ?

   Sir To. Go, write it in a martial hand ; be curst and
brief ; it is no matter how witty, so it be eloquent and
full of invention : taunt him with the license of ink :
if thou thou'st him some thrice, it shall not be amiss ;
and as many lies as will lie in thy sheet of paper,
although the sheet were big enough for the bed of Ware
in England, set 'em down : go, about it. Let there be
gall enough in thy ink, though thou write with a
goose-pen, no matter : about it.

50   *Sir And.* Where shall I find you ?

---

26. *Like an icicle . . . beard.* It was a Dutchman who discovered
      Northern Nova Zembla at the close of the sixteenth century.
30. *Brownists,* a sect of Puritans founded by a certain Robert
      Brown.
31. *Politician,* Crafty schemer.   41. *Curst,* Sharp-spoken.
46. *Bed of Ware.* This great oak bedstead, able to hold a dozen
      persons, was formerly kept at an inn at Ware, Hertford-
      shire.
48. *Gall,* Bitterness. Ox-gall was formerly used in the manufacture
      of ink, so there is a play on the word here.

Sir To. We'll call thee at the cubiculo: go.

[*Exit* Sir Andrew.

Fab. This is a dear manakin to you, Sir Toby.

Sir To. I have been dear to him, lad, some two thousand strong, or so.

Fab. We shall have a rare letter from him: but you'll not deliver't?

Sir To. Never trust me, then; and by all means stir on the youth to an answer. I think oxen and wain-ropes cannot hale them together. For Andrew, if 60 he were opened, and you find so much blood in his liver as will clog the foot of a flea, I'll eat the rest of the anatomy.

Fab. And his opposite, the youth, bears in his visage no great presage of cruelty.

[*Enter* Maria.]

Sir To. Look, where the youngest wren of nine comes.

Mar. If you desire the spleen, and will laugh your-selves into stitches, follow me. Yond gull Malvolio is turned heathen, a very renegado; for there is no 70 Christian, that means to be saved by believing rightly, can ever believe such impossible passages of grossness. He's in yellow stockings.

Sir To. And cross-gartered?

Mar. Most villanously; like a pedant that keeps a school i' the church. I have dogged him, like his murderer. He does obey every point of the letter that I dropped to betray him: he does smile his face into

---

51. *Cubiculo*, Room.   59. *Wain-ropes*, Cart-ropes.
67. *Spleen.* "By the spleen we are moved to laugh, by the gall we be wroth, by the heart we be wise, by the brain we feel, by the liver we love."—Eng. trans. of Bartholomæus.
69. *Renegado*, one who turns against the principles of his faith.
74. *Pedant*, Schoolmaster. It is said that, while the grammar-school at Stratford was being repaired, classes were held in the neighbouring church.

more lines than is in the new map with the augmenta-
tion of the Indies : you have not seen such a thing as
80 'tis.   I can hardly forbear hurling things at him.   I
know my lady will strike him : if she do, he'll smile
and take't for a great favour.

   Sir To. Come, bring us, bring us where he is.

                                   [*Exeunt.*

SCENE III

A street.

[*Enter* SEBASTIAN *and* ANTONIO.]

   Seb. I would not by my will have troubled you ;
But, since you make your pleasure of your pains,
I will no further chide you.
   Ant. I could not stay behind you : my desire,
More sharp than filed steel, did spur me forth ;
And not all love to see you, though so much
As might have drawn one to a longer voyage,
But jealousy what might befall your travel,
Being skilless in these parts ; which to a stranger,
10 Unguided and unfriended, often prove
Rough and unhospitable : my willing love,
The rather by these arguments of fear,
Set forth in your pursuit.
   Seb.   My kind Antonio,
I can no other answer make but thanks,
And thanks, and ever thanks ; too oft good turns
Are shuffled off with such uncurrent pay :
But, were my worth as is my conscience firm,
You should find better dealing.   What's to do ?
Shall we go see the reliques of this town ?

78, 79. *The new map . . . Indies.* The phrase explains itself. Prob-
    ably the map was one drawn by a certain Mollineux, and
    found in some copies of Hakluyt's *Voyages.*
8. *Jealousy*, Suspicious fear.   16. *Uncurrent*, Valueless.
19. *Reliques*, Relics, such as old monuments, etc.

20   *Ant.* To-morrow, sir : best first go see your lodging.
    Seb. I am not weary, and 'tis long to night :
I pray you, let us satisfy our eyes
With the memorials and the things of fame
That do renown this city.
    Ant.   Would you'ld pardon me ;
I do not without danger walk these streets :
Once, in a sea-fight, 'gainst the count his galleys
I did some service ; of such note indeed,
That were I ta'en here it would scarce be answer'd.
    Seb. Belike you slew great number of his people ?
30   *Ant.* The offence is not of such a bloody nature
Albeit the quality of the time and quarrel
Might well have given us bloody argument.
It might have since been answer'd in repaying
What we took from them ; which, for traffic's sake,
Most of our city did : only myself stood out ;
For which, if I be lapsed in this place,
I shall pay dear.
    Seb.   Do not then walk too open.
    Ant. It doth not fit me. Hold, sir, here's my purse.
In the south suburbs, at the Elephant,
40 Is best to lodge : I will bespeak our diet,
Whiles you beguile the time and feed your knowledge
With viewing of the town : there shall you have me.
    Seb. Why I your purse ?
    Ant. Haply your eye shall light upon some toy
You have desire to purchase ; and your store,
I think, is not for idle markets, sir.
    Seb. I'll be your purse-bearer and leave you
For an hour.
    Ant.   To the Elephant.
    Seb.   I do remember. [*Exeunt.*

28. *Answered*, Atoned for.   29. *Belike*, Perhaps.
31. *Albeit*, Although. 32. *Bloody argument*, Matter for bloodshed.
34. *Traffic*, Trade. 36. *Lapsed*, Taken.

SCENE IV

OLIVIA's *garden*.

[*Enter* OLIVIA *and* MARIA.]

Oli. I have sent after him : he says he'll come ;
How shall I feast him ? what bestow of him ?
For youth is bought more oft than begg'd or borrow'd.
I speak too loud.
Where is Malvolio ? he is sad and civil,
And suits well for a servant with my fortunes ·
Where is Malvolio ?

Mar. He's coming, madam ; but in very strange
manner. He is, sure, possessed, madam.

10   *Oli.* Why, what's the matter ? does he rave ?

Mar. No, madam, he does nothing but smile : your
ladyship were best to have some guard about you, if he
come ; for, sure, the man is tainted in's wits.

Oli. Go call him hither. [*Exit* MARIA.] I am as
    mad as he,
If sad and merry madness equal be.

[*Re-enter* MARIA, *with* MALVOLIO.]

How now, Malvolio !

Mal. Sweet lady, ho, ho.

Oli. Smilest thou ?
I sent for thee upon a sad occasion.

20   *Mal.* Sad, lady ! I could be sad ; this does make
some obstruction in the blood, this cross-gartering ;
but what of that ? if it please the eye of one, it is
with me as the very true sonnet is, " Please one, and
please all."

Oli. Why, how dost thou, man ? what is the matter
with thee ?

Mal. Not black in my mind, though yellow in my

5. *Sad*, Grave.
23. *Sonnet*, used in Elizabethan English for any kind of short poem.

71

legs. It did come to his hands, and commands shall
be executed: I think we do know the sweet Roman
30 hand.

Oli. Wilt thou go to bed, Malvolio?

Mal. To bed! ay, sweetheart.

Oli. God comfort thee! Why dost thou smile so
and kiss thy hand so oft?

Mar. How do you, Malvolio?

Mal. At your request! yes; nightingales answer
daws.

Mar. Why appear you with this ridiculous boldness
before my lady?

40 *Mal.* "Be not afraid of greatness:" 'twas well
writ.

Oli. What meanest thou by that, Malvolio?

Mal. "Some are born great,"—

Oli. Ha!

Mal. "Some achieve greatness,"—

Oli. What sayest thou?

Mal. "And some have greatness thrust upon them."

Oli. Heaven restore thee!

Mal. "Remember who commended thy yellow
50 stockings,"—

Oli. Thy yellow stockings!

Mal. "And wished to see thee cross-gartered."

Oli. Cross-gartered!

Mal. "Go to, thou art made, if thou desirest to be
so;"—

Oli. Am I made?

Mal. "If not, let me see thee a servant still."

Oli. Why, this is very midsummer madness.

[*Enter* Servant.]

Ser. Madam, the young gentleman of the Count
60 Orsino's is returned: I could hardly entreat him
back: he attends your ladyship's pleasure.

---

29. *Roman hand.* In the sixteenth century the Italian and Roman
    style of handwriting became fashionable in England.

Oli. I'll come to him. [*Exit* Servant.] Good Maria, let this fellow be looked to. Where's my cousin Toby? Let some of my people have a special care of him: I would not have him miscarry for the half of my dowry.   [*Exeunt* OLIVIA *and* MARIA.

Mal. O, ho! do you come near me now? no worse man than Sir Toby to look to me! This concurs directly with the letter: she sends him on purpose,
70 that I may appear stubborn to him; for she incites me to that in the letter. "Cast thy humble slough," says she; "be opposite with a kinsman, surly with servants; let thy tongue tang with arguments of state; put thyself into the trick of singularity;" and consequently sets down the manner how; as, a sad face, a reverend carriage, a slow tongue, in the habit of some sir of note, and so forth. I have limed her; but it is Jove's doing, and Jove make me thankful! And when she went away now, "Let this fellow be looked
80 to:" fellow! not Malvolio, nor after my degree, but fellow. Why, everything adheres together, that no dram of a scruple, no scruple of a scruple, no obstacle, no incredulous or unsafe circumstance—What can be said? Nothing that can be can come between me and the full prospect of my hopes. Well, Jove, not I, is the doer of this, and he is to be thanked.

[*Re-enter* MARIA, *with* SIR TOBY *and* FABIAN.]

Sir To. Which way is he, in the name of sanctity? If all the devils of hell be drawn in little, and Legion himself possessed him, yet I'll speak to him.
90 *Fab.* Here he is, here he is. How is't with you, sir? how is't with you, man?
Mal. Go off; I discard you: let me enjoy my private: go off.
Mar. Lo, how hollow the fiend speaks within him!

65. *Miscarry*, Come to harm.
77. *Limed her*, Caught her, as a bird is trapped with bird-lime.

Did not I tell you ?   Sir Toby, my lady prays you to
have a care of him.

   Mal. Ah, ha ! does she so ?

   Sir To. Go to, go to ; peace, peace ; we must deal
gently with him : let me alone.   How do you, Mal-
100 volio ?   how is't with you ?   What man ! defy the
devil : consider, he's an enemy to mankind.

   Mal. Do you know what you say ?

   Mar. La you, an you speak ill of the devil,
how he takes it at heart !   Pray God, he be not
bewitched !   My lady would not lose him for more
than I'll say.

   Mal. How now, mistress !

   Mar. O Lord !

   Sir To. Prithee, hold thy peace : this is not the
110 way : do you not see you move him ? let me alone
with him.

   Fab. No way but gentleness ; gently, gently : the
fiend is rough, and will not be roughly used.

   Sir To. Why, how now, my bawcock ! how dost
thou, chuck ?

   Mal. Sir !

   Sir To. Ay, Biddy, come with me.   What, man !
'tis not for gravity to play at cherry-pit with Satan :
hang him, foul collier !

120   *Mar.* Get him to say his prayers, good Sir Toby, get
him to pray.

   Mal. My prayers, minx !

   Mar. No, I warrant you, he will not hear of godli-
ness.

   Mal. Go, hang yourselves all ! you are idle shallow
things : I am not of your element : you shall know
more hereafter.   [*Exit.*

   Sir To. Is't possible ?

---

114. *Bawcock* (fine fellow) ; 115. *Chuck* (chick), colloquial terms of
    endearment, most unsuitable for the staid Malvolio.
118. *Cherry-pit,* a game in which cherry-stones are pitched into a
    hole.

Fab. If this were played upon a stage now, I could
130 condemn it as an improbable fiction.

Sir To. His very genius hath taken the infection of
the device, man.

Mar. Nay, pursue him now, lest the device take air
and taint.

Fab. Why, we shall make him mad indeed.

Mar. The house will be the quieter.

Sir To. Come, we'll have him in a dark room and
bound. My niece is already in the belief that he's
mad : we may carry it thus, for our pleasure and his
140 penance, till our very pastime, tired out of breath,
prompt us to have mercy on him : at which time we
will bring the device to the bar and crown thee for a
finder of madmen. But see, but see.

[*Enter* SIR ANDREW.]

Fab. More matter for a May morning.

Sir And. Here's the challenge, read it : I warrant
there's vinegar and pepper in't.

Fab. Is't so saucy ?

Sir And. Ay, is't, I warrant him : do but read.

Sir To. Give me. [*Reads*] " Youth, whatsoever
150 thou art, thou art but a scurvy fellow."

Fab. Good and valiant.

Sir To. [*Reads*] " Wonder not, nor admire not in
thy mind, why I do call thee so, for I will show thee no
reason for't."

Fab. A good note ; that keeps you from the blow of
the law.

Sir To. [*Reads*] " Thou comest to the Lady Olivia,
and in my sight she uses thee kindly : but thou liest
in thy throat : that is not the matter I challenge
160 thee for."

131. *Genius*, the guardian spirit formerly supposed to dwell with
      man and control his actions.
133. *Take air and taint*, Become exposed and ruined.
152. *Admire*, Be surprised.

Fab. Very brief, and to exceeding good sense—less.

Sir To. [*Reads*] " I will waylay thee going home ; where if it be thy chance to kill me,"—

Fab. Good.

Sir To. [*Reads*] " Thou killest me like a rogue and a villain."

Fab. Still you keep o' the windy side of the law : good.

Sir To. [*Reads*] " Fare thee well ; and God have
170 mercy upon one of our souls ! He may have mercy upon mine ; but my hope is better, and so look to thyself. Thy friend, as thou usest him, and thy sworn enemy, Andrew Aguecheek." If this letter move him not, his legs cannot ; I'll give 't him.

Mar. You may have very fit occasion for't : he is now in some commerce with my lady, and will by and by depart.

Sir To. Go, Sir Andrew ; scout me for him at the corner of the orchard like a bum-baily : so soon as
180 ever thou seest him, draw ; and as thou drawest, swear horrible ; for it comes to pass oft that a terrible oath, with a swaggering accent sharply twanged off. gives manhood more approbation than ever proof itself would have earned him. Away !

Sir And. Nay, let me alone for swearing.   [*Exit.*

Sir To. Now will not I deliver his letter : for the behaviour of the young gentleman gives him out to be of good capacity and breeding ; his employment between his lord and my niece confirms no less : there-
190 fore this letter, being so excellently ignorant, will breed no terror in the youth : he will find it comes from a clodpole. But, sir, I will deliver his challenge by word of mouth ; set upon Aguecheek a notable

167. *Windy side o' the law*, The safe side, the advantageous side, as
    that of the boat sailing to windward in a race.
176. *Commerce*, Intercourse.   176. *By and by*, Immediately.
179. *Bum-baily*, The " bound-bailiff " (who arrested for debt).
183. *Approbation*, Confirmation.
192. *Clodpole*, Blockhead.

report of valour ; and drive the gentleman, as I know
his youth will aptly receive it, into a most hideous
opinion of his rage, skill, fury and impetuosity. This
will so fright them both that they will kill one another by the look, like cockatrices.

        [*Re-enter* OLIVIA, *with* VIOLA.]

    Fab. Here he comes with your niece : give them
200 way till he take leave, and presently after him.
    Sir To. I will meditate the while upon some horrid
message for a challenge.

        [*Exeunt* SIR TOBY, FABIAN, *and* MARIA.

    Oli. I have said too much unto a heart of stone,
And laid mine honour too unchary out :
There's something in me that reproves my fault ;
But such a headstrong potent fault it is,
That it but mocks reproof.
    Vio. With the same 'haviour that your passion
        bears
Goes on my master's grief.
210   *Oli.* Here, wear this jewel for me, 'tis my picture ;
Refuse it not ; it hath no tongue to vex you ;
And I beseech you come again to-morrow.
What shall you ask of me that I'll deny,
That honour saved may upon asking give ?
    Vio. Nothing but this ; your true love for my
        master.
    Oli. How with mine honour may I give him that
Which I have given to you ?
    Vio.   I will acquit you.
    Oli. Well, come again to-morrow : fare thee well :
A fiend like thee might bear my soul to hell.   [*Exit.*

        [*Re-enter* SIR TOBY *and* FABIAN.]

220   *Sir To.* Gentleman, God save thee.
    Vio. And you, sir.
    Sir To. That defence thou hast, betake thee to't :

  198. *Cockatrice,* a serpent which could inflict death by its glance.

77

of what nature the wrongs are thou hast done him, I know not : but thy intercepter, full of despite, bloody as the hunter, attends thee at the orchard-end : dismount thy tuck, be yare in thy preparation, for thy assailant is quick, skilful and deadly.

Vio. You mistake, sir ; I am sure no man hath any quarrel to me : my remembrance is very free and clear 230 from any image of offence done to any man.

Sir To. You'll find it otherwise, I assure you : therefore, if you hold your life at any price, betake you to your guard ; for your opposite hath in him what youth, strength, skill and wrath can furnish man withal.

Vio. I pray you, sir, what is he ?

Sir To. He is knight, dubbed with unhatched rapier and on carpet consideration ; but he is a devil in private brawl : souls and bodies hath he divorced 240 three ; and his incensement at this moment is so implacable, that satisfaction can be none but by pangs of death and sepulchre. Hob, nob, is his word ; give't or take't.

Vio. I will return again into the house and desire some conduct of the lady. I am no fighter. I have heard of some kind of men that put quarrels purposely on others, to taste their valour : belike this is a man of that quirk.

Sir To. Sir, no ; his indignation derives itself out 250 of a very competent injury : therefore, get you on and give him his desire. Back you shall not to the house, unless you undertake that with me which with as much

---

224. *Despite*, Spite, malice.   226. *Tuck*, Rapier.
226. *Yare*, Swift.   233. *Opposite*, Adversary.
237, 238. *Dubbed ... consideration.* The "carpet-knight" received his title, not for prowess in warfare, but for some other reason ; the sword which dubbed or touched him on the shoulder was not dented with the blows of battle, but unhacked (unhatched) ; and he was not knighted on the field, but on the carpet of some royal apartment.
242. *Hob, nob,* To have or not to have, come what may.
248. *Quirk*, Humour.   250. *Competent*, Sufficient.

safety you might answer him : therefore, on, or strip
your sword stark naked ; for meddle you must, that's
certain, or forswear to wear iron about you.

Vio. This is as uncivil as strange.   I beseech you,
do me this courteous office, as to know of the knight
what my offence to him is : it is something of my
negligence, nothing of my purpose.

260 *Sir To.* I will do so.   Signor Fabian, stay you by
this gentleman till my return.   [*Exit.*

Vio. Pray you, sir, do you know of this matter ?

Fab. I know the knight is incensed against you, even
to a mortal arbitrement ; but nothing of the circumstance more.

Vio. I beseech you, what manner of man is he ?

Fab. Nothing of that wonderful promise, to read
him by his form, as you are like to find him in the
proof of his valour.   He is, indeed, sir, the most skil-
270 ful, bloody and fatal opposite that you could possibly
have found in any part of Illyria.   Will you walk towards him ?   I will make your peace with him if I can.

Vio. I shall be much bound to you for't : I am one
that had rather go with sir priest than sir knight : I
care not who knows so much of my mettle.   [*Exeunt.*

[*Re-enter* SIR TOBY, *with* SIR ANDREW.]

Sir To. Why, man, he's a very devil ; I have not
seen such a firago.   I had a pass with him, rapier,
scabbard and all, and he gives me the stuck in with
such a mortal motion, that it is inevitable ; and on
280 the answer, he pays you as surely as your feet hit the
ground they step on.   They say he has been fencer to
the Sophy.

Sir And. Plague on't, I'll not meddle with him.

---

264. *Mortal arbitrement*, Decision by death.
277. *Firago*, Virago, a bold fierce woman.   Perhaps the term is
    jestingly used by Sir Toby because this youth has struck him
    as womanish.

277. *Pass*, Bout.	278. *Stuck*, Thrust.
279. *Motion*, Suggestion.	280. *Answer*, Return thrust.

Sir To. Ay, but he will not now be pacified: Fabian can scarce hold him yonder.

Sir And. Plague on't, an I thought he had been valiant and so cunning in fence, I'ld have seen him damned ere I'ld have challenged him. Let him let the matter slip, and I'll give him my horse, grey 290 Capilet.

Sir To. I'll make the motion: stand here, make a good show on't: this shall end without the perdition of souls. [*Aside*] Marry, I'll ride your horse as well as I ride you.

[*Re-enter* FABIAN *and* VIOLA.]

[*To Fab.*] I have his horse to take up the quarrel: I have persuaded him the youth's a devil.

Fab. He is as horribly conceited of him: and pants and looks pale, as if a bear were at his heels.

Sir To. [*To Vio.*] There's no remedy, sir; he will 300 fight with you for's oath sake: marry, he hath better bethought him of his quarrel, and he finds that now scarce to be worth talking of: therefore draw, for the supportance of his vow; he protests he will not hurt you.

Vio. [*Aside*] Pray God defend me! A little thing would make me tell them how much I lack of a man.

Fab. Give ground, if you see him furious.

Sir To. Come, Sir Andrew, there's no remedy; the gentleman will, for his honour's sake, have one bout 310 with you; he cannot by the duello avoid it: but he has promised me, as he is a gentleman and a soldier, he will not hurt you. Come on; to't.

Sir And. Pray God, he keep his oath!

Vio. I do assure you, 'tis against my will.

[*They draw.*

297. *Is as horribly conceited of*, Has an equally horrible notion of.
310. *Duello*, The laws of duelling.

[*Enter* Antonio.]

Ant. Put up your sword. If this young gentleman
Have done offence, I take the fault on me ;
If you offend him, I for him defy you.
  Sir To. You, sir ! why, what are you ?
  Ant. One, sir, that for his love dares yet do more
320 Than you have heard him brag to you he will.
  Sir To. Nay, if you be an undertaker, I am for you.
                                        [*They draw.*
                [*Enter* Officers.]

Fab. O good Sir Toby, hold ! here come the officers.
  Sir To. I'll be with you anon.
  Vio. Pray, sir, put your sword up, if you please.
  Sir And. Marry, will I, sir ; and, for that I pro-
mised you, I'll be as good as my word : he will bear
you easily and reins well.
  First Off. This is the man ; do thy office.
  Sec. Off. Antonio, I arrest thee at the suit of Count
330 Orsino.
  Ant. You do mistake me, sir.
  First Off. No, sir, no jot ; I know your favour well,
Though now you have no sea-cap on your head.
Take him away : he knows I know him well.
  Ant. I must obey. [*To Vio.*] This comes with
    seeking you :
But there's no remedy ; I shall answer it.
What will you do, now my necessity
Makes me to ask you for my purse ? It grieves me
Much more for what I cannot do for you
340 Than what befalls myself. You stand amazed ;
But be of comfort.
  Sec. Off. Come, sir, away.
  Ant. I must entreat of you some of that money.
  Vio. What money, sir ?

323. *Anon*, At once.

For the fair kindness you have show'd me here,
And, part, being prompted by your present trouble,
Out of my lean and low ability
I'll lend you something : my having is not much ;
I'll make division of my present with you :
350 Hold, there's half my coffer.
    Ant.   Will you deny me now ?
Is't possible that my deserts to you
Can lack persuasion ?   Do not tempt my misery,
Lest that it make me so unsound a man
As to upbraid you with those kindnesses
That I have done for you.
    Vio.   I know of none ;
Nor know I you by voice or any feature :
I hate ingratitude more in a man
Than lying, vainness, babbling, drunkenness
Or any taint of vice whose strong corruption
360 Inhabits our frail blood.
    Ant.   O heavens themselves !
    Sec. Off. Come, sir, I pray you, go.
    Ant. Let me speak a little.   This youth that you
        see here
I snatch'd one half out of the jaws of death,
Relieved him with such sanctity of love,
And to his image, which methought did promise
Most venerable worth, did I devotion.
    First Off. What's that to us ?   The time goes by :
        away !
    Ant. But O how vile an idol proves this god !
Thou hast, Sebastian, done good feature shame.
370 In nature there's no blemish but the mind ;
None can be call'd deform'd but the unkind :
Virtue is beauty, but the beauteous evil
Are empty trunks o'erflourish'd by the devil.
    First Off. The man grows mad : away with him !
        Come, come, sir.

373. *O'erflourished*, Adorned all over, here with decorative designs
    in carving.

Ant. Lead me on. [*Exit with Officers.*

Vio. Methinks his words do from such passion fly,
That he believes himself : so do not I.
Prove true, imagination, O. prove true,
That I, dear brother, be now ta'en for you !
380 *Sir To.* Come hither, knight ; come hither, Fabian :
we'll whisper o'er a couplet or two of most sage saws.

Vio. He named Sebastian : I my brother know
Yet living in my glass : even such and so
In favour was my brother, and he went
Still in this fashion, colour, ornament,
For him I imitate : O, if it prove,
Tempests are kind and salt waves fresh in love. [*Exit.*

Sir To. A very dishonest paltry boy, and more a
coward than a hare : his dishonesty appears in leaving
390 his friend here in necessity and denying him ; and for
his cowardship, ask Fabian.

Fab. A coward, a most devout coward, religious in it.

Sir And. I'll after him again and beat him.

Sir To. Do ; cuff him soundly, but never draw thy
sword.

Sir And. An I do not,— [*Exit.*

Fab. Come, let's see the event.

Sir To. I dare lay any money 'twill be nothing yet.
[*Exeunt.*

ACT IV

SCENE I

Before OLIVIA'S *house.*

[*Enter* SEBASTIAN *and* CLOWN.]

Clo. Will you make me believe that I am not sent
for you ?

Seb. Go to, go to, thou art a foolish fellow :
Let me be clear of thee.

Clo. Well held out, i' faith ! No, I do not know
you ; nor I am not sent to you by my lady, to bid you
come speak with her ; nor your name is not Master
Cesario ; nor this is not my nose neither.   Nothing
that is so is so.

10   *Seb.* I prithee, vent thy folly somewhere else ·
Thou know'st not me.

Clo. Vent my folly ! he has heard that word on
some great man and now applies it to a fool.   Vent
my folly !   I am afraid this great lubber, the world,
will prove a cockney.   I prithee now, ungird thy
strangeness and tell me what I shall vent to my lady :
shall I vent to her that thou art coming ?

Seb. I prithee, foolish Greek, depart from me :

10. *Vent*, Utter.
15. *Cockney*, an effeminate, affected person.   This word has under-
    gone interesting changes of meaning (petted child—affected
    person—townsman—Londoner).
16. *Strangeness*, Distant manner.
18. *Greek*, a gay light-hearted person, as in our phrase " as merry
    as a grig," where " grig " stands for Greek.   The use of the
    word rose from the Roman idea of the Greeks as a pleasure-
    loving people.

84

There's money for thee : if you tarry longer,
20 I shall give worse payment.

Clo. By my troth, thou hast an open hand.   These
wise men that give fools money get themselves a good
report—after fourteen years' purchase.

[*Enter* Sir Andrew Sir Toby, *and* Fabian.]

Sir And. Now, sir, have I met you again ? there's
for you.

Seb. Why, there's for thee, and there, and there.
Are all the people mad ?

Sir To. Hold, sir, or I'll throw your dagger o'er the
house.

30   *Clo.* This will I tell my lady straight : I would not
be in some of your coats for two pence.   [*Exit.*

Sir To. Come on, sir ; hold.

Sir And. Nay, let him alone : I'll go another way
to work with him ; I'll have an action of battery
against him, if there be any law in Illyria : though I
struck him first, yet it's no matter for that.

Seb. Let go thy hand.

Sir To. Come, sir, I will not let you go.   Come, my
young soldier, put up your iron : you are well fleshed ;
40 come on.

Seb. I will be free from thee.   What wouldst thou
     now ?
If thou darest tempt me further, draw thy sword.

Sir To. What, what ?   Nay, then I must have an
ounce or two of this malapert blood from you.

[*Enter* Olivia.]

Oli. Hold, Toby ; on thy life I charge thee, hold !
Sir To. Madam !

23. *Fourteen years' purchase*, Paying dearly for it. *Purchase*, or the
      marketable value of land, was calculated on the sum of its
      annual rentals for so many years—generally twelve.
39. *Iron*, Sword.
39. *You are well fleshed*, You have tasted blood enough.
44. *Malapert*, Impudent.

Oli. Will it be ever thus ?   Ungracious wretch,
Fit for the mountains and the barbarous caves,
Where manners ne'er were preach'd ! out of my sight !
50 Be not offended, dear Cesario.
Rudesby, be gone !
        [Exeunt Sir Toby, Sir Andrew, *and* Fabian.
                I prithee, gentle friend,
Let thy fair wisdom, not thy passion, sway
In this uncivil and unjust extent
Against thy peace.   Go with me to my house,
And hear thou there how many fruitless pranks
This ruffian hath botch'd up, that thou thereby
Mayst smile at this : thou shalt not choose but go :
Do not deny.   Beshrew his soul for me,
He started one poor heart of mine in thee.
60   *Seb.* What relish is in this ? how runs the stream ?
Or I am mad, or else this is a dream :
Let fancy still my sense in Lethe steep ;
If it be thus to dream, still let me sleep !
    Oli. Nay, come, I prithee ; would thou'ldst be
      ruled by me !
    Seb. Madam, I will.
    Oli.   O, say so, and so be ! *[Exeunt.*

SCENE II

Olivia's *house.*

[*Enter* Maria *and* Clown.]

Mar. Nay, I prithee, put on this gown and this
beard ; make him believe thou art Sir Topas the
curate : do it quickly ; I'll call Sir Toby the whilst.
                        [Exit.

51. *Rudesby,* Boorish fellow.
53. *Extent,* Violent attack ; a legal term.
56. *Botched up,* lit. Patched up, brought about.
2. *Sir Topas.* The title Sir was formerly applied to clergymen.
    Most of these had taken the B.A. degree, holders of which
    were styled dominus (sir) at the universities.

Clo. Well, I'll put it on, and I will dissemble myself in't ; and would I were the first that ever dissembled in such a gown.   I am not tall enough to become the function well, nor lean enough to be thought a good student ; but to be said an honest man and a good housekeeper goes as fairly as to say a careful man and 10 a great scholar.   The competitors enter.

[*Enter* SIR TOBY *and* MARIA.]

Sir To. Jove bless thee, master Parson.

Clo. Bonos dies, Sir Toby : for, as the old hermit of Prague, that never saw pen and ink, very wittily said to a niece of King Gorboduc, " That that is is " : so I, being master Parson, am master Parson : for, what is " that " but " that," and " is " but " is " ?

Sir To. To him, Sir Topas.

Clo. What, ho, I say ! peace in this prison !

Sir To. The knave counterfeits well ; a good knave.

20 *Mal.* [*Within*] Who calls there ?

Clo. Sir Topas the curate, who comes to visit Malvolio the lunatic.

Mal. Sir Topas, Sir Topas, good Sir Topas, go to my lady.

Clo. Out, hyperbolical fiend ! how vexest thou this man ! talkest thou nothing but of ladies ?

Sir To. Well said, master Parson.

Mal. Sir Topas, never was man thus wronged : good Sir Topas, do not think I am mad : they have laid 30 me here in hideous darkness.

Clo. Fie, thou dishonest Satan ! I call thee by the most modest terms ; for I am one of those gentle ones that will use the devil himself with courtesy : sayest thou that house is dark ?

---

10. *Competitors*, Confederates.
12. *Hermit of Prague*, an invention of Feste's.
14. *King Gorboduc*, an early British king.   The first English
        tragedy in blank verse was called *Gorboduc* (1561).
19. *Knave*, Boy.   32. *Modest*, Moderate.

Mal. As hell, Sir Topas.

Clo. Why, it hath bay windows transparent as barricadoes, and the clerestories toward the south north are as lustrous as ebony ; and yet complainest thou of obstruction ?

40 *Mal.* I am not mad, Sir Topas : I say to you, this house is dark.

Clo. Madman, thou errest : I say, there is no darkness but ignorance ; in which thou art more puzzled than the Egyptians in their fog.

Mal. I say, this house is dark as ignorance, though ignorance were as dark as hell ; and I say, there was never man thus abused.   I am no more mad than you are : make the trial of it in any constant question.

Clo. What is the opinion of Pythagoras concerning 50 wild fowl ?

Mal. That the soul of our grandam might haply inhabit a bird.

Clo. What thinkest thou of his opinion ?

Mal. I think nobly of the soul, and no way approve his opinion.

Clo. Fare thee well.   Remain thou still in darkness: thou shalt hold the opinion of Pythagoras ere I will allow of thy wits, and fear to kill a woodcock, lest thou dispossess the soul of thy grandam.   Fare thee 60 well.

Mal. Sir Topas, Sir Topas !

Clo. Nay, I am for all waters.

Sir To. My most exquisite Sir Topas !

Mar. Thou mightst have done this without thy beard and gown : he sees thee not.

Sir To. To him in thine own voice, and bring me word how thou findest him : I would we were well rid

---

37. *Clerestory,* a row of windows above the arches of the nave, to be seen in Gothic architecture.
47. *Abused,* Ill-used.
49. *Pythagoras,* a Greek philosopher who taught the doctrine of the transmigration of souls—*i.e.* that after death the souls of human beings may pass into the bodies of animals.

of this knavery. If he may be conveniently delivered,
I would he were, for I am now so far in offence with
70 my niece that I cannot pursue with any safety this
sport to the upshot. Come by-and-by to my chamber.

[*Exeunt* SIR TOBY *and* MARIA.

Clo. [*Singing*] " Hey, Robin, jolly Robin,
        Tell me how thy lady does."

Mal. Fool !

Clo. " My lady is unkind, perdy."

Mal. Fool !

Clo. " Alas, why is she so ? "

Mal. Fool, I say !

Clo. " She loves another "—Who calls, ha ?

80 *Mal.* Good fool, as ever thou wilt deserve well at
my hand, help me to a candle, and pen, ink and paper :
as I am a gentleman, I will live to be thankful to
thee for't.

Clo. Master Malvolio ?

Mal. Ay, good fool.

Clo. Alas, sir, how fell you besides your five wits ?

Mal. Fool, there was never man so notoriously
abused : I am as well in my wits, fool, as thou art.

Clo. But as well ? then you are mad indeed, if you
90 be no better in your wits than a fool.

Mal. They have here propertied me ; keep me in
darkness, send ministers to me, asses, and do all they
can to face me out of my wits.

Clo. Advise you what you say ; the minister is here.
Malvolio, Malvolio, thy wits the heavens restore !
endeavour thyself to sleep, and leave thy vain bibble-
babble.

Mal. Sir Topas !

Clo. Maintain no words with him, good fellow.

---

75. *Perdy*, a mild oath (Fr. *pardieu*).
86. *Five wits*, the powers of the mind (" common wit, imagination,
    fantasy, estimation, memory ").
91. *Propertied me*, Treated me as a mere chattel.
94. *Advise you*, Be careful.

100 Who, I, sir ? not I, sir. God be wi' you, good Sir
Topas. Marry, amen. I will, sir, I will.

Mal. Fool, fool, fool, I say !

Clo. Alas, sir, be patient. What say you, sir ? I
am shent for speaking to you.

Mal. Good fool, help me to some light and some
paper : I tell thee, I am as well in my wits as any man
in Illyria.

Clo. Well-a-day that you were, sir !

Mal. By this hand, I am. Good fool, some ink,
110 paper and light ; and convey what I will set down to
my lady : it shall advantage thee more than ever the
bearing of letter did.

Clo. I will help you to't. But tell me true, are you
not mad indeed ? or do you but counterfeit ?

Mal. Believe me, I am not ; I tell thee true.

Clo. Nay, I'll ne'er believe a madman till I see his
brains. I will fetch you light and paper and ink.

Mal. Fool, I'll requite it in the highest degree : I
prithee, be gone.

120   *Clo.* [*Singing*] I am gone, sir,
                And anon, sir,
            I'll be with you again,
                In a trice,
                Like to the old Vice,
            Your need to sustain ;

            Who, with dagger of lath,
            In his rage and his wrath,
                Cries, ah, ha ! to the devil :
            Like a mad lad,
130   Pare thy nails, dad ;
                Adieu, good man devil.   [*Exit.*

104. *Shent*, Scolded.   118. *Requite*, Reward.
124. *Vice.* In the old Morality play comic relief was provided by the
        Devil, whose make-up included a hair suit, a great red nose,
        and long claws, and the Vice, a buffoon who wore a long
        motley coat and carried a wooden dagger. One of the
        Vice's tricks was to attempt to cut the Devil's nails with
        this dagger.

SCENE III

OLIVIA'S *garden.*

[*Enter* SEBASTIAN.]

Seb. This is the air ; that is the glorious sun ;
This pearl she gave me, I do feel't, and see't ;
And though 'tis wonder that enwraps me thus,
Yet 'tis not madness.   Where's Antonio, then ?
I could not find him at the Elephant :
Yet there he was ; and there I found this credit,
That he did range the town to seek me out.
His counsel now might do me golden service ;
For though my soul disputes well with my sense,
10 That this may be some error, but no madness,
Yet doth this accident and flood of fortune
So far exceed all instance, all discourse,
That I am ready to distrust mine eyes
And wrangle with my reason that persuades me
To any other trust but that I am mad
Or else the lady's mad ; yet, if 'twere so,
She could not sway her house, command her followers,
Take and give back affairs and their dispatch
With such a smooth, discreet and stable bearing
20 As I perceive she does : there's something in't
That is deceivable.   But here the lady comes.

[*Enter* OLIVIA *and* Priest.]

Oli. Blame not this haste of mine.   If you mean well,
Now go with me and with this holy man
Into the chantry by : there, before him,
And underneath that consecrated roof,

6. *Credit*, General opinion.   12. *Instance*, Example, precedent.
12. *Discourse*, Reasoning.   15. *Trust*, Belief.

Plight me the full assurance of your faith ;
That my most jealous and too doubtful soul
May live at peace.   He shall conceal it
Whiles you are willing it shall come to note,
30 What time we will our celebration keep
According to my birth.   What do you say ?
   Seb. I'll follow this good man, and go with you
And, having sworn truth, ever will be true.
   Oli. Then lead the way, good father ; and heavens
    so shine,
That they may fairly note this act of mine !   [*Exeunt.*

ACT V

SCENE I

Before OLIVIA'S *house*.

[*Enter* CLOWN *and* FABIAN.]

Fab. Now, as thou lovest me, let me see his letter.
Clo. Good Master Fabian, grant me another request.
Fab. Any thing.
Clo. Do not desire to see this letter.
Fab. This is, to give a dog, and in recompense desire my dog again.

[*Enter* DUKE, VIOLA, CURIO, *and* Lords.]

Duke. Belong you to the Lady Olivia, friends?
Clo. Ay, sir; we are some of her trappings.
Duke. I know thee well: how dost thou, my good
10 fellow?
Clo. Truly, sir, the better for my foes and the worse for my friends.
Duke. Just the contrary; the better for thy friends.
Clo. No, sir, the worse.
Duke. How can that be?
Clo. Marry, sir, they praise me and make an ass of me; now my foes tell me plainly I am an ass: so that by my foes, sir, I profit in the knowledge of my-self, and by my friends I am abused: so that, con-

19. *Abused,* Deceived.

20 clusions to be as kisses, if your four negatives make
your two affirmatives, why then, the worse for my
friends and the better for my foes.

Duke. Why, this is excellent.

Clo. By my troth, sir, no ; though it please you to
be one of my friends.

Duke. Thou shalt not be the worse for me : there's
gold.

Clo. But that it would be double-dealing, sir, I
would you could make it another.

30 *Duke.* O, you give me ill counsel.

Clo. Put your grace in your pocket, sir, for this
once, and let your flesh and blood obey it.

Duke. Well, I will be so much a sinner, to be a
double-dealer : there's another.

Clo. Primo, secundo, tertio, is a good play ; and
the old saying is, the third pays for all : the triplex,
sir, is a good tripping measure ; or the bells of Saint
Bennet, sir, may put you in mind ; one, two, three.

Duke. You can fool no more money out of me at this
40 throw : if you will let your lady know I am here to
speak with her, and bring her along with you, it may
awake my bounty further.

Clo. Marry, sir, lullaby to your bounty till I come
again.   I go, sir ; but I would not have you to think
that my desire of having is the sin of covetousness :
but, as you say, sir, let your bounty take a nap, I will
awake it anon.   [*Exit.*

Vio. Here comes the man, sir, that did rescue me.

[*Enter* ANTONIO *and* Officers.]

Duke. That face of his I do remember well ;
50 Yet, when I saw it last, it was besmear'd
As black as Vulcan in the smoke of war :

35. *Primo, secundo, tertio,* First, second, third. The phrase may
     have been used in playing some dicing game.
37. *Saint Bennet,* a church opposite the Globe Theatre, destroyed
     in the Great Fire of London.

A bawbling vessel was he captain of,
For shallow draught and bulk unprizable ;
With which such scathful grapple did he make
With the most noble bottom of our fleet,
That very envy and the tongue of loss
Cried fame and honour on him.   What's the matter ?

   First Off. Orsino, this is that Antonio
That took the Phœnix and her fraught from Candy ;
30 And this is he that did the Tiger board,
When your young nephew Titus lost his leg :
Here in the streets, desperate of shame and state,
In private brabble did we apprehend him.

   Vio. He did me kindness, sir, drew on my side ;
But in conclusion put strange speech upon me :
I know not what 'twas but distraction.

   Duke. Notable pirate ! thou salt-water thief !
What foolish boldness brought thee to their mercies,
Whom thou, in terms so bloody and so dear,
70 Hast made thine enemies ?

   Ant.   Orsino, noble sir,
Be pleased that I shake off these names you give me :
Antonio never yet was thief or pirate,
Though I confess, on base and ground enough,
Orsino's enemy.   A witchcraft drew me hither :
That most ingrateful boy there by your side,
From the rude sea's enraged and foamy mouth
Did I redeem ; a wreck past hope he was :
His life I gave him and did thereto add
My love, without retention or restraint,
80 All his in dedication ; for his sake
Did I expose myself, pure for his love,
Into the danger of this adverse town ;
Drew to defend him when he was beset :
Where being apprehended, his false cunning,
Not meaning to partake with me in danger,
Taught him to face me out of his acquaintance,

---

52. *Bawbling,* Paltry.   53. *Unprizable,* Valueless.
54. *Scathful,* Harmful. 55. *Bottom,* Ship.   59. *Fraught,* Cargo.

And grew a twenty years' removed thing
While one would wink ; denied me mine own purse,
Which I had recommended to his use
90 Not half an hour before.
  Vio.   How can this be ?
  Duke. When came he to this town ?
  Ant. To-day, my lord ; and for three months before,
No interim, not a minute's vacancy,
Both day and night did we keep company.

     [*Enter* Olivia *and* Attendants.]

  Duke. Here comes the countess : now heaven walks
   on earth.
But for thee, fellow ; fellow, thy words are madness :
Three months this youth hath tended upon me ;
But more of that anon.   Take him aside.
  Oli. What would my lord, but that he may not
   have,
100 Wherein Olivia may seem serviceable ?
Cesario, you do not keep promise with me.
  Vio. Madam !
  Duke. Gracious Olivia,—
  Oli. What do you say, Cesario ?   Good my lord,—
  Vio. My lord would speak ; my duty hushes me.
  Oli. If it be aught to the old tune, my lord,
It is as fat and fulsome to mine ear
As howling after music.
  Duke.   Still so cruel !
  Oli. Still so constant, lord.
110 *Duke.* What, to perverseness ? you uncivil lady,
To whose ingrate and unauspicious altars
My soul the faithfull'st offerings hath breathed out
That e'er devotion tender'd !   What shall I do ?
  Oli. Even what it please my lord, that shall become
   him.
  Duke. Why should I not, had I the heart to do it,

    107. *Fat,* Distasteful.

Like to the Egyptian thief at point of death,
Kill what I love ?—a savage jealousy
That sometime savours nobly.   But hear me this :
Since you to non-regardance cast my faith,
120 And that I partly know the instrument
That screws me from my true place in your favour,
Live you the marble-breasted tyrant still ;
But this your minion, whom I know you love,
And whom, by heaven I swear, I tender dearly,
Him will I tear out of that cruel eye,
Where he sits crowned in his master's spite.
Come, boy, with me ; my thoughts are ripe in mis-
      chief :
I'll sacrifice the lamb that I do love,
To spite a raven's heart within a dove.
130   *Vio.* And I, most jocund, apt and willingly,
To do you rest, a thousand deaths would die.
   Oli. Where goes Cesario ?
   Vio.   After him I love
More than I love these eyes, more than my life,
More, by all mores, than e'er I shall love wife.
If I do feign, you witnesses above
Punish my life for tainting of my love !
   Oli. Ay me, detested ! how am I beguiled !
   Vio. Who does beguile you ? who does do you
      wrong ?
   Oli. Hast thou forgot thyself ? is it so long ?
140 Call forth the holy father.
   Duke.   Come, away !
   Oli. Whither, my lord ?   Cesario, husband, stay.
   Duke. Husband !

116. *The Egyptian thief.* Thyamis, the captain of a band of robbers.
    He captured the lovers Theagenes and Chariclea, and him-
    self fell in love with the maiden.   When attacked by another
    band of robbers he attempted to kill her, that she might be
    his companion in the next life, but, in the darkness of the
    cave where she was shut up, he slew another woman for
    her, and she escaped.
123. *Minion*, Favourite.   124. *Tender*, Hold dear.

Oli.   Ay, husband : can he that deny ?
Duke. Her husband, sirrah !
Vio.   No, my lord, not I.
Oli. Alas, it is the baseness of thy fear
That makes thee strangle thy propriety :
Fear not, Cesario ; take thy fortunes up ;
Be that thou know'st thou art, and then thou art
As great as that thou fear'st.

[*Enter* Priest.]

                       O, welcome, father !
Father, I charge thee, by thy reverence,
150 Here to unfold, though lately we intended
To keep in darkness what occasion now
Reveals before 't is ripe, what thou dost know
Hath newly pass'd between this youth and me.
    Priest. A contract of eternal bond of love,
Confirm'd by mutual joinder of your hands,
Attested by the holy close of lips,
Strengthen'd by interchangement of your rings ;
And all the ceremony of this compact
Seal'd in my function, by my testimony :
160 Since when, my watch hath told me, toward **my**
        grave
I have travell'd but two hours.
    Duke. O thou dissembling cub ! what wilt thou be
When time hath sow'd a grizzle on thy case ?
Or will not else thy craft so quickly grow,
That thine own trip shall be thine overthrow ?
Farewell, and take her ; but direct thy feet
Where thou and I henceforth may never meet.
    Vio. My lord, I do protest—
    Oli.   O, do not swear !
Hold little faith, though thou hast too much fear.

145. *Propriety*, Identity.
151. *Occasion*, the pressing demand of the moment.
163. *Case*, Skin.

98

[*Enter* SIR ANDREW.]

170 *Sir And.* For the love of God, a surgeon ! Send one presently to Sir Toby.

Oli. What's the matter ?

Sir And. He has broke my head across and has given Sir Toby a bloody coxcomb too : for the love of God, your help ! I had rather than forty pound I were at home.

Oli. Who has done this, Sir Andrew ?

Sir And. The count's gentleman, one Cesario : we took him for a coward, but he's the very devil in-
180 cardinate.

Duke. My gentleman, Cesario ?

Sir And. 'Od's lifelings, here he is ! You broke my head for nothing ; and that that I did, I was set on to do 't by Sir Toby.

Vio. Why do you speak to me ? I never hurt you : You drew your sword upon me without cause ; But I bespake you fair, and hurt you not.

Sir And. If a bloody coxcomb be a hurt, you have hurt me : I think you set nothing by a bloody
190 coxcomb.

[*Enter* SIR TOBY *and* CLOWN.]

Here comes Sir Toby halting ; you shall hear more : but if he had not been in drink, he would have tickled you othergates than he did.

Duke. How now, gentleman ! how is 't with you ?

Sir To. That's all one : has hurt me, and there's the end on 't. Sot, didst see Dick surgeon, sot ?

Clo. O, he's drunk, Sir Toby, an hour agone ; his eyes were set at eight i' the morning.

Sir To. Then he's a rogue, and a passy measures
200 pavin : I hate a drunken rogue.

Oli. Away with him ! Who hath made this havoc
with them ?

Sir And. I'll help you, Sir Toby, because we'll be
dressed together.

Sir To. Will you help ? an ass-head and a coxcomb
and a knave, a thin-faced knave, a gull !

Oli. Get him to bed, and let his hurt be look'd to.

[*Exeunt* CLOWN, FABIAN, SIR TOBY, *and*
SIR ANDREW.

[*Enter* SEBASTIAN.]

Seb. I am sorry, madam, I have hurt your kinsman ;
But, had it been the brother of my blood,
210 I must have done no less with wit and safety.
You throw a strange regard upon me, and by that
I do perceive it hath offended you :
Pardon me, sweet one, even for the vows
We made each other but so late ago.

Duke. One face, one voice, one habit, and two
persons,
A natural perspective, that is and is not !

Seb. Antonio, O my dear Antonio !
How have the hours rack'd and tortured me,
Since I have lost thee !

220   *Ant.* Sebastian are you ?

Seb.   Fear'st thou that, Antonio ?

Ant. How have you made division of yourself ?
An apple, cleft in two, is not more twin

---

199. *Passy measures pavin.* "Set at eight," according to Dr. Naylor,
    brings to Sir Toby's mind these two dances, both of which
    were set in " strains " of eight bars each. *Passy-measures*,
    pazzamezzo, *pavin*, or pavane, both stately slow-moving
    Italian dances. As has been pointed out, the line of prog-
    ress of a drunken man may well suggest a parody of the
    steps of the pazzamezzo, " two single and a double forward,
    and two single syde, reprynce back."

216. *Perspective*, a glass cut in such a way as to produce an optical
    delusion.

Than these two creatures.   Which is Sebastian ?

    Oli. Most wonderful !

    Seb. Do I stand there ?   I never had a brother ;
Nor can there be that deity in my nature,
Of here and everywhere.   I had a sister,
Whom the blind waves and surges have devour'd.
Of charity, what kin are you to me ?
230 What countryman ? what name ? what parentage ?

    Vio. Of Messaline : Sebastian was my father ;
Such a Sebastian was my brother too,
So went he suited to his watery tomb :
If spirits can assume both form and suit
You come to fright us.

    Seb.   A spirit I am indeed ;
But am in that dimension grossly clad
Which from my birth I did participate.
Were you a woman, as the rest goes even,
I should my tears let fall upon your cheek,
240 And say " Thrice welcome, drowned Viola ! "

    Vio. My father had a mole upon his brow.

    Seb. And so had mine.

    Vio. And died that day when Viola from her birth
Had number'd thirteen years.

    Seb. O, that record is lively in my soul !
He finished indeed his mortal act
That day that made my sister thirteen years.

    Vio. If nothing lets to make us happy both
But this my masculine usurp'd attire,
250 Do not embrace me till each circumstance
Of place, time, fortune, do cohere and jump
That I am Viola : which to confirm,
I'll bring you to a captain in this town,
Where lie my maiden weeds ; by whose gentle help
I was preserved to serve this noble count.

---

236. *Dimension,* Bodily shape.   245. *Record,* Recollection.
248. *Lets,* Hinders.   251. *Jump,* Agree together.
254. *Weeds,* Garments.

All the occurrence of my fortune since
Hath been between this lady and this lord.

   Seb. [*To* Olivia] So comes it, lady, you have been
     mistook :

But nature to her bias drew in that.
260 You would have been contracted to a maid ;
Nor are you therein, by my life, deceived,
You are betroth'd both to a maid and man.

   Duke. Be not amazed ; right noble is his blood.
If this be so, as yet the glass seems true,
I shall have share in this most happy wreck.
[*To* Viola] Boy, thou hast said to me a thousand
    times
Thou never shouldst love woman like to me.

   Vio. And all these sayings will I over-swear ;
And all those swearings keep as true in soul
270 As doth that orbed continent the fire
That severs day from night.

   Duke.   Give me thy hand ;
And let me see thee in thy woman's weeds.

   Vio. The captain that did bring me first on shore
Hath my maid's garments : he upon some action
Is now in durance, at Malvolio's suit,
A gentleman, and follower of my lady's.

   Oli. He shall enlarge him : fetch Malvolio hither :
And yet, alas, now I remember me,
They say, poor gentleman, he's much distract.

   [*Re-enter* Clown *with a letter, and* Fabian.]

280 A most extracting frenzy of mine own
From my remembrance clearly banish'd his.
How does he, sirrah ?

   Clo. Truly, madam, he holds Belzebub at the stave's
end as well as man in his case may do : has here writ

---

259. *Bias,* Natural tendency. The word belongs to the game of
    bowls, the bias being the weight on one side of the bowl,
    making it incline a certain way.
270. *Orbed continent,* The sun.   275. *Durance,* Prison.
277. *Enlarge,* Set free.   280. *Extracting,* Absorbing.

a letter to you; I should have given 't you to-day
morning, but as a madman's epistles are no gospels, so
it skills not much when they are delivered.

Oli. Open 't, and read it.

Clo. Look then to be well edified when the fool
290 delivers the madman. [*Reads*] " By the Lord,
madam,"—

Oli. How now ! art thou mad ?

Clo. No, madam, I do but read madness : an your
ladyship will have it as it ought to be, you must
allow Vox.

Oli. Prithee, read i' thy right wits.

Clo. So do I, madonna ; but to read his right wits is
to read thus : therefore perpend, my princess, and
give ear.

300 *Oli.* Read it you, sirrah. [*To* FABIAN.

Fab. [*Reads*] " By the Lord, madam, you wrong me,
and the world shall know it : though you have put me
into darkness and given your drunken cousin rule over
me, yet have I the benefit of my senses as well as your
ladyship.   I have your own letter that induced me to
the semblance I put on : with the which I doubt not
but to do myself much right, or you much shame.
Think of me as you please.   I leave my duty a little
unthought of and speak out of my injury.

310 THE MADLY-USED MALVOLIO."

Oli. Did he write this ?

Clo. Ay, madam.

Duke. This savours not much of distraction.

Oli. See him deliver'd, Fabian ; bring him hither.

[*Exit* FABIAN.

My lord, so please you, these things further thought
on,

To think me as well a sister as a wife,

287. *It skills not,* It does not matter.
290. *Delivers,* Utters the words of.
295. *Vox,* The (right) voice. Feste begins to read the letter with
the voice and gesture of a madman.
298. *Perpend,* Consider.

One day shall crown the alliance on 't, so please you,
Here at my house and at my proper cost.

    Duke. Madam, I am most apt to embrace your offer.
320 [*To* VIOLA] Your master quits you ; and for your
        service done him,
So much against the mettle of your sex,
So far beneath your soft and tender breeding,
And since you call'd me master for so long,
Here is my hand : you shall from this time be
Your master's mistress.

    Oli.   A sister ! you are she.

[*Re-enter* FABIAN, *with* MALVOLIO.]

    Duke. Is this the madman ?
    Oli.   Ay, my lord, this same.
How now, Malvolio !

    Mal.   Madam, you have done me wrong,
Notorious wrong.

    Oli.   Have I, Malvolio ? no.

    Mal. Lady, you have. Pray you, peruse that letter.
330 You must not now deny it is your hand :
Write from it, if you can, in hand or phrase ;
Or say 't is not your seal, not your invention :
You can say none of this : well, grant it then
And tell me, in the modesty of honour,
Why you have given me such clear lights of favour,
Bade me come smiling and cross-garter'd to you,
To put on yellow stockings and to frown
Upon Sir Toby and the lighter people ;
And, acting this in an obedient hope,
340 Why have you suffer'd me to be imprison'd,
Kept in a dark house, visited by the priest,
And made the most notorious geck and gull
That e'er invention play'd on ? tell me why.

318. *Proper,* Own.   319. *Apt,* Ready.
320. *Quits you,* Sets you free from service.
321. *Mettle,* Natural spirit.
334. *Modesty,* Plain unexaggerated statement.   342. *Geck,* Dupe.

Oli. Alas, Malvolio, this is not my writing,
Though, I confess, much like the character :
But out of question 'tis Maria's hand.
And now I do bethink me, it was she
First told me thou wast mad ; thou camest in smiling
And in such forms which here were presupposed
Upon thee in the letter.   Prithee, be content :
This practice hath most shrewdly pass'd upon thee ;
But when we know the grounds and authors of it,
Thou shalt be both the plaintiff and the judge
Of thine own cause.

Fab.   Good madam, hear me speak,
And let no quarrel nor no brawl to come
Taint the condition of this present hour,
Which I have wonder'd at.   In hope it shall not,
Most freely I confess, myself and Toby
Set this device against Malvolio here,
Upon some stubborn and uncourteous parts
We had conceived against him : Maria writ
The letter at Sir Toby's great importance ;
In recompense whereof he hath married her.
How with a sportful malice it was follow'd,
May rather pluck on laughter than revenge ;
If that the injuries be justly weigh'd
That have on both sides pass'd.

Oli. Alas, poor fool, how have they baffled thee !

Clo. Why, "some are born great, some achieve greatness, and some have greatness thrown upon them." I was one, sir, in this interlude; one Sir Topas, sir ; but that's all one. "By the Lord, fool, I am not mad." But do you remember ? "Madam, why laugh you at such a barren rascal ? an you smile not, he's gagged ;" and thus the whirligig of time brings in his revenges.

345. *Character*, Handwriting.   351. *Practice*, Plot.
351. *Shrewdly*, Cruelly.
362. *Importance*, Importunity, eager request.
368. *Baffled*, Treated shamefully.   371. *Interlude*, Little play.
375. *Whirligig*, Spinning top.

Mal. I'll be revenged on the whole pack of you.

[*Exit.*

Oli. He hath been most notoriously abused.

Duke. Pursue him, and entreat him to a peace :
380 He hath not told us of the captain yet :
When that is known and golden time convents,
A solemn combination shall be made
Of our dear souls.   Meantime, sweet sister,
We will not part from hence.   Cesario, come ;
For so you shall be, while you are a man ;
But when in other habits you are seen,
Orsino's mistress and his fancy's queen.

[*Exeunt all, except* CLOWN.

Clo. [*Sings*]
When that I was and a little tiny boy,
    With hey, ho, the wind and the rain,
390 A foolish thing was but a toy,
    For the rain it raineth every day.

But when I came to man's estate,
    With hey, ho, etc.
'Gainst knaves and thieves men shut their gate,
    For the rain, etc.

But when I came, alas ! to wive,
    With hey, ho, etc.
By swaggering could I never thrive,
    For the rain, etc.

400 But when I came unto my beds,
    With hey, ho, etc.
With toss-pots still had drunken heads,
    For the rain, etc.

381. *Convents,* Is convenient.   387. *Fancy,* Love.
Except Clown (*stage direction*).   Often, at the end of a play on the
    Elizabethan stage, the clown would entertain the audience
    with a song and dance.   This performance was called the
    " jig."

A great while ago the world begun,
  With hey, ho, etc.
But that's all one, our play is done,
  And we'll strive to please you every day.   [*Exit.*

HELPS TO FURTHER STUDY

SHAKESPEARE'S LIFE AND ENVIRONMENT
(To 1600)

SHAKESPEARE'S was not the lot of the genius un-recognized in his lifetime and lauded after his death. When *Twelfth Night* was written, in 1600 or 1601, he had been thirteen or fourteen years in London, and his position was assured. Not only was he well off as far as money goes, but his supremacy, both as play-wright and poet, was established.

It is uncertain which company of players he had joined when, "a youth unknown to fame," he had left Stratford-on-Avon and come to London, but, in the 'nineties of the sixteenth century, he was one of the "Lord Chamberlain's men," who, after the acces-sion of James I. in 1603, were honoured with the title of the "King's Players." The two playhouses in Shoreditch with which he was probably first associ-ated, the *Theatre* and the *Curtain*, might seem bare and uncomfortable places to a modern audience, but in that age they excited great wonder and enthusiasm for their "beauty" and "gorgeousness." When he had been in London for a few years the *Rose* and *Newington Butts* sprang up, and he acted in both these, but the playhouse with which he had most con-cern was the famous *Globe*, built on Bankside in 1599 by the Burbages from the fabric of the demolished

Theatre. It was new when the Prologue of *Henry V.* alludes to it :

> " May we cram
> Within this wooden O the very casques
> That did affright the air at Agincourt ? "

There is no detailed record of the actual appearance of this famous old theatre. It had stood for only fourteen years, when, during a performance of *Henry VIII.*, " set forth with many extraordinary circumstances of pomp and majesty, even to the matting on the stage," the discharge of two small cannon set fire to the thatch of the roof, and in a short time the whole theatre was burnt to the ground. It was rebuilt in the following year. A sketch of this second *Globe* appears in a contemporary map, and from this, from Shakespeare's touch of description, and from what is known generally of the architecture of the sixteenth and seventeenth century theatres, it is possible to gain an idea of what the original *Globe* looked like.

There was considerable difference between the private theatre, such as *Blackfriars*, in which Shakespeare, towards the end of his career, had shares, and the public one. The first *Blackfriars* was part of a private house fitted up by the master of the choir school at Windsor as a little theatre, where his boys might give performances under his management. Seating accommodation was limited, and the audience was smaller and, apparently, of less mixed a character than that of the public theatre. The architecture of the latter is reminiscent of the inn-yard where, before they had houses of their own, the players would bring their movable " pageant " or wooden stage and act their drama to those who looked from the windows and balconies of the inn buildings or crowded round the stage to watch them. Indeed, the " pit " of the theatre was at first called the " yard " ; the boxes were the " rooms " ; and a signboard, resembling that of the tavern, indicated the name of the theatre. That of the *Globe* showed Hercules bearing the world on his shoulders.

The public theatre was built of wood, and only partially roofed, the rush-strewn " yard " being exposed to the weather. The stage or *scaffold* was what is called an *apron stage*, differing from the *picture stage* common in present-day theatres in that it projected into the pit. Such a stage allows of no curtain, and the entrances and exits of the actors are not protected, as it were, by wings. There was no scenery in the modern sense, though a " painted cloth " or piece of arras was occasionally used. At the back of the stage was a wooden erection, hollowed out so that it might serve the purpose of a bed, or an arbour, or a tomb, while its upper part might be the city walls, or a balcony, or any place for which the direction " aloft " is given. Stage furniture, though not elaborate, was sufficient—chairs, tables, thrones, mossy banks, cauldrons, chariots, and so on, appear to have been easily available. A musicians' gallery was in the rear of the stage, but its exact position is unknown. There was much music, and no lack of realistic noise —storms, the galloping of horses' feet, alarums to battle, flourishes of trumpets, firing of cannon. Little or no attempt was made to dress the play according to period, but the costume worn was magnificent. The dramatist Heywood got less for one play than was spent on the gown of the heroine— and this heroine was impersonated by a boy. Actresses were unknown on the public stage before the Restoration—all Shakespeare's women's parts were played by boys with their voices yet unbroken.

Plays were acted not only in the theatres, but, on occasion, in the royal palaces and the houses of noblemen, in the universities and the Inns of Court. A barrister, John Manningham, has a note in his diary about the play of *Twelfth Night*, produced in the Middle Temple Hall in February 1602.

HELPS TO FURTHER STUDY

Shakespeare was praised as an actor, called " excellent in the quality he professes," and although he played small parts, such as the Ghost in *Hamlet* and old Adam in *As You Like It*, they are parts that demand imaginative rendering. In 1594 he was among those of his company summoned to play at Greenwich Palace before the queen, whose patronage of the arts was not a mere pose sustained by flattery, but the result of genuine taste and learning. Tradition declares him to have been singled out for royal favour, and this is substantiated by Ben Jonson's praise " in memory of my beloved Master William Shakespeare "—

> " Sweet Swan of Avon ! what a sight it were
> To see thee in our waters yet appear,
> And make those flights upon the banks of Thames,
> That so did take Eliza and our James."

As poet and playwright he was acknowledged supreme. In 1598, Francis Meres, a divine and schoolmaster, published his *Palladis Tamia* (Treasury of Wit), in which he praised Shakespeare as " most excellent " in both tragedy and comedy, and declared that " the Muses would speak Shakespeare's fine filed phrase, if they could speak English." As for his poems and " sugred sonnets among his private friends," Meres declares that they prove "that the sweet witty soul of Ovid lives in mellifluous and honey-tongued Shakespeare."

Towards the end of the sixteenth century Shakespeare was living in Southwark, then famous for its fine inns, at one of which, the Tabard, Chaucer and his fellow-pilgrims had spent the night before setting out for Canterbury. His lodging was near the *Globe*

Quality, the technical term for the actor's profession.
His private friends. It was not unusual for poets to circulate their sonnets in manuscript among their friends. Shakespeare's were not published until 1609.

and the building known as the *Bear Garden*, devoted to bear-baiting, and apparently the scene of much rowdy behaviour. He would look over the " sweet Thames," the great " silent highway " of London, gay with sailing ships, private barges, and the boats of the watermen, to St. Paul's Church, with its square central tower, and to pleasant gabled houses, with stairs leading to the water. His plays showed that he loved order, comfort, and elegance, and most probably he lived and dressed well, as a successful actor could.

> " England affords those glorious vagabonds,
>   That carried erst their fardles on their backs,
>   Coursers to ride on through the gazing streets,
>   Sweeping it in their glaring satin suits,
>   And pages to attend their masterships."

From his plays, his salary as an actor, and his shares in the *Globe* theatre, he had a good income. Sir Sidney Lee has calculated that it would be over £600, and, as the purchasing power of money at that time was eight times what it was in our century before the war, this stands for a very fair sum.

While the young man from the Midlands prospered thus in London, fortune had been against his family at home. In the summer of 1596, his little boy Hamnet died, and was buried in Stratford parish church. The two remaining children of Shakespeare's boyhood marriage with Anne Hathaway were both girls —Susanna was now thirteen, and Judith, Hamnet's twin, eleven. During the year of his son's death Shakespeare returned to his native town. His father, John Shakespeare, a dealer in various sorts of agricultural produce, had once known prosperity, holding high civic offices (burgess or town councillor, chamberlain of the borough, with the duty of auditing

England, etc. So complains a character in the University play, *The Return from Parnassus.*

municipal accounts, alderman, bailiff or mayor), and playing an important part in the affairs of the town. But before Shakespeare left Stratford this prosperity was on the decline ; he owed various sums of money, had been forced to mortgage one property of Mary Arden, his wife, and sell another, and, failing to attend council meetings regularly, was deprived of the dignity of alderman. For years things had gone from bad to worse, but his son's return marked a change in his fortunes. No more is heard of the importunity of creditors, and, in the autumn of 1596, John Shakespeare made application to the College of Heralds for a coat of arms, finally obtained, though not until three years later. In the following year his son bought for himself the Great House which had been built by Sir Hugh Clopton in Henry VII.'s reign, renamed it New Place, and set about improving it as a residence, repairing the parts that had fallen into ruin, and planning to convert the " great garden " into an orchard.

During Shakespeare's absence his wife as well as his father had apparently been in difficulties, for she had borrowed money from a Thomas Whittington, who had been her father's shepherd. When this man died, at the beginning of the next century, his executor was directed to claim the money from Shakespeare and give it to the poor.

What we know of Shakespeare contradicts the popular notion that genius is essentially unpractical in business matters. He knew how to make money, how to manage and spend it, and provided for the common needs of a decent and comely life as strength and sanity will. What were the adventures, the delights, and the sufferings of his spirit his work alone can tell us—the plays indirectly, the sonnets, perhaps, directly. It has been supposed that their story of broken friendship and unhappy love is Shakespeare's own story, and that the " dark lady " whom he addresses with the passion of mingled love and hate was Mary Fitton, maid of honour to the queen. Certainly it is very difficult to believe that they do not express some poignant personal experience. Wordsworth declares, " With this key Shakespeare unlocked his heart," but many of the poet's biographers agree with Browning's retort, " Did Shakespeare ?   If so, the less Shakespeare he ! "

CHIEF RECORDED EVENTS OF THE LIFE OF SHAKESPEARE

(*For Reference*)

1564. On 26th April, William Shakespeare baptized at the parish church of Stratford-on-Avon. He is the first son and third child of *John Shakespeare*, a trader in agricultural produce, and holder of various important municipal offices in Stratford (four years after the poet's birth he was " bailiff " or mayor of the town), and of *Mary Arden*, who came of good yeoman stock.

1582. At the age of eighteen Shakespeare marries *Ann Hathaway*, eight years older than himself, daughter of a farmer of Shottery, a little village near Stratford.   It is generally supposed that the marriage was not a happy one. Much has been made of the passage in *Twelfth Night*, where the Duke gives advice to Cesario (see page 50, l. 30), of Shakespeare's long absences from Stratford, and of the fact that the sole bequest to his wife in his will is " the second best bed with its furniture."

1583. Birth of Shakespeare's daughter Susanna.

1584. Birth of his twin children, Judith and Hamnet. The boy died at the age of eleven.

1592. The poet and dramatist, Robert Greene, in a pamphlet called *A Groatsworth of Wit Bought with a Million of Repentance*, attacks a young actor as " an upstart crow, beautified with our feathers, that with his tiger's heart wrapped in a player's hide supposes he is as well able to bombast out a blank verse as the best of you : and being an absolute Johannes factotum is, in his own conceit, the only Shakescene in the country." Obviously Shakespeare is meant, and, by this time, he must have left Stratford for London and the theatre. Later, the publisher of this pamphlet apologizes for Greene's ill-natured attack, and speaks of Shakespeare as " excellent in the quality he professes."

1593, 1594. Publication of the poems *Venus and Adonis* and *Lucrece,* both dedicated to the Earl of Southampton.

1594. Shakespeare mentioned as one of the actors of the Lord Chamberlain's company. He plays before the queen at Greenwich.

1596. The College of Heralds grants John Shakespeare a coat of arms, obtained three years later. He is known to have been in financial difficulties before this date. It is thought probable that his son returned to Stratford in this year, and established the fortunes of the family on a firmer basis.

1597. Shakespeare buys New Place at Stratford.

1598. Francis Meres publishes his *Palladis Tamia* (Treasury of Wit), in which he praises Shakespeare as the greatest dramatist of the time. He mentions his narrative poems, his sonnets, six comedies (*Two Gentlemen of Verona, Errors, Love's Labour's Lost, Love's Labour's Won, Midsummer Night's Dream,* and *Merchant of*

Love's Labour's Won : perhaps *All's Well that Ends Well.*

Venice), and six tragedies (*Richard II., Richard III., Henry IV., King John, Titus, Romeo and Juliet*).

1599. Globe Theatre built. Shakespeare becomes a shareholder in the receipts of this theatre.

1601. Death of John Shakespeare, from whom his son inherits the houses in Henley Street now known as " Shakespeare's House."

1602. Shakespeare purchases arable land near Stratford.

1603. The Lord Chamberlain's company receives its license from James I., and is henceforth known as the King's Company or the King's Servants.

Theatres closed on account of the plague, and the court leaves London.

1604. Shakespeare is one of the actors chosen to walk in the procession accompanying the king on his entry into London.

1605. He buys a moiety (portion) of the tithes of Stratford, but this investment does not prove a very satisfactory one.

1607. His elder daughter, Susanna, marries Dr. John Hall. Their daughter Elizabeth was the only grandchild Shakespeare lived to see. She was the last surviving direct descendant of the poet.

1609. The Burbages, who had leased the *Blackfriars* Theatre, bought out the lessee. Shakespeare is one of the players who becomes a shareholder (profits much less than at the *Globe*).

1610. Shakespeare purchases pastoral land, to add to that bought in 1602.

1611. He settles at Stratford.

1616. His younger daughter, Judith, marries Thomas Quiney, son of one of his old friends. Of their three sons, one died in infancy, the other two in young manhood.

Death of Shakespeare (23rd April). He is

buried in Stratford parish church, and over his grave are inscribed these lines :

" Good friend, for Jesus' sake forbeare
   To dig the dust enclosed heare ;
   Bleste be the man that spares these stones,
   And curst be he that moves these bones."

THE WORK OF SHAKESPEARE

c. 1590–1599. Plays :—*Love's Labour's Lost, The Two Gentlemen of Verona, the Comedy of Errors, Romeo and Juliet, Henry VI., Richard III., Richard II., Titus Andronicus, The Merchant of Venice, King John, A Midsummer Night's Dream, The Taming of the Shrew, The Merry Wives of Windsor, Henry V., Much Ado About Nothing, As You Like It.*

   Poems :—*Venus and Adonis, Lucrece,* the Sonnets.

1600–1610. *Julius Cæsar, Twelfth Night, Hamlet, Troilus and Cressida, All's Well that Ends Well, Othello, Measure for Measure, Macbeth, King Lear, Timon of Athens, Pericles, Antony and Cleopatra, Coriolanus.*

1610–1611. *Cymbeline, The Winter's Tale, The Tempest, Henry VIII.*

THE SONGS IN "TWELFTH NIGHT"

MUSIC played so important a part in the life of the England of the sixteenth and seventeenth centuries that it is not surprising that there should be many allusions to it, and opportunities for its introduction, in the plays of Shakespeare. Not only is there the martial music of the alarum, and the stirring sennet or tucket, there is the gay music of masque and revelry, the romantic music of the garden of Belmont, the fantastic airy music of the reconciliation of the fairy king and queen in the wood near Athens, the enchantment of sounds and sweet airs on the island of *The Tempest*, the tranquil harmony which soothed the tortured mind of an old mad king. And there are the songs. In no play is there more of music than in *Twelfth Night*. The first Act opens with music, and with one of the loveliest poems in the praise of sweet sound in the English language (the other is spoken by Lorenzo to Jessica in Portia's garden), and the last Act ends with a song.

" O Mistress mine," printed in 1599, a year before *Twelfth Night* is judged to have been written, is supposed not to have been composed in connection with the play, but to have been introduced into it ; but, whether or not this is the case, it is difficult to believe that it was written by any one but Shakespeare. Its setting is of special interest, being one of the only two (the other is " It was a lover and his lass ") of Shakespeare's own songs published during his lifetime. It appears in Morley's *First Booke of Consort*

Lessons, made by divers exquisite Authors for six instruments to play together, the Treble-Lute, the Pandora, the Citterne, the Bass Viol, the Flute, and Treble Viol.

O Mis-tress mine, where are you roam-ing?

O stay and hear! your true love's com-ing,

That can sing both high and low Trip

- - no fur- ther, pret-ty sweet - ing,

Jour - neys end in - - - lov-ers meet - ing, Ev-

- - 'ry wise man's son doth know.

Feste's "When that I was a little tiny boy," the burden of which is sung by the Fool in *Lear*, may have been a popular contemporary song. The following

TWELFTH NIGHT

tune belongs to theatrical tradition ; there is no
record of the original setting.

When that I was a little ti-ny boy With a heigh ho the

wind and the rain A fool-ish thing was but a toy, For the

rain it rain-eth ev - ry day, With a heigh ho ! the

wind and the rain And the rain it rain - eth ev - ry day.

Of the various post-Shakespearian airs composed for
" Come away, Death," that by Dr. Arne (eighteenth
century) is the most popular.

Come a-way, come a-way, death, and in sad cy - press

let me be laid ; Fly a-way, fly a - way, breath ; I am

slain, I am slain by a fair cru-el maid. My shroud of white stuck

all with yew, O pre-pare it, O pre-pare it;

My part of death no one so true, no one so true Did

share it. Not a flow'r, not a flow'r sweet,

On my black cof-fin let there be strown; Not a friend,

not a friend greet My poor corpse, where my bones shall be thrownA

thou - sand thou - sand sighs to save, Lay me, O,

lay me where Sad true lov-er nev - er find my grave To

weep there, to weep there.

TWELFTH NIGHT

The snatches of song that occur in Act II. are from popular Elizabethan ballads. The "catch" (see page 45) was so arranged that each singer called the other "knave" in turn. These are the words and the tune:

When Maria reproaches the revellers for their "caterwauling," Sir Toby remarks that Malvolio is a "Peg of Ramsey" and "three merry men be we." He has a wag's delight in contriving the most inappropriate nicknames and terms of endearment for the solemn pompous steward (later on come "bawcock" and "chuck," and "Biddy"). This is how "Peg o' Ramsey" goes, with its seventeenth-century tune:

HELPS TO FURTHER STUDY

This is the song of the " Three Merry Men " :

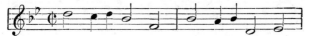

Three mer-ry men, and three mer-ry men, and

three mer-ry men be we, I in the wood and

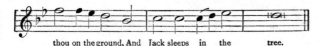

thou on the ground, And Jack sleeps in the tree.

" Farewell, dear heart," is a parody of an Elizabethan song called " Corydon's Farewell to Phillis." These are the first two verses :

" Farewell, dear love ; since thou wilt needs begone,
Mine eyes do show, my life is almost done.
Nay I will never die, so long as I can spie
There be many mo, though that she doe goe.
There be many mo, I fear not ;
Why then let her goe, I care not.

Farewell, farewell ; since this I find is true,
I will not spend more time in wooing you ;
But I will seek elsewhere, if I may find love there ;
Shall I bid her goe and spare not ?
O no, no, no, I dare not."

This is the early seventeenth-century tune to which Sir Toby and Feste sing their lines :

(Sir Toby)

Fare-well dear heart since I must needs be

TWELFTH NIGHT

(Feste)

gone, His eyes do show his days are al - most

(Sir Toby)

done, But I will nev - er, nev - er, nev - er

(Feste)

die. Oh then, Sir To - by, then, oh then, you lie.

This is the old song of Robin and his lady with which Feste teases Malvolio in Act IV. :

Hey, Rob - in, jol - ly Rob - in, Tell me how thy la - dy does,

Hey, Rob - in, jol - ly Rob - in, Tell me how thy la - dy does.

DATE AND SOURCES OF THE PLAY

MOST scholars agree that Shakespeare wrote *Twelfth Night* in 1600 or 1601, for the festivity of Twelfth Night (6th January, the Epiphany and the twelfth day after Christmas). It is not included in the comedies mentioned by Meres (see page 115) in his *Palladis Tamia*, published in 1598, and in February 1602 John Manningham noted its performance in the Hall of the Middle Temple. The new map spoken of by Maria when she describes Malvolio's smiling face was printed in 1599 or 1600; Feste's complaint that " words are very rascals since bonds disgraced them " is supposed by some to refer to certain restrictions on the stage ordered by the Privy Council in 1600 and 1601. The evidence of style and metre also points to the early seventeenth century as the time of the composition of the play.

(Fairly advanced students should notice the outstanding differences in the style of Shakespeare's early and later plays, such as in the use of prose and rhymed lines ; the use of classical allusion ; and the changes in the structure of the blank verse, with the increase of the " run-on " line, the extra syllable at the cæsura, etc.)

Manningham, commenting on the play, says it is " much like the *Comedy of Errors* or *Menechmi* in Plautus ; but most like and near to that in Italian called *Inganni*." There are two Italian plays called *Gl'Inganni* (The Cheats), and one called *Gl'Ingannati* (The Cheated), which have some similarity to *Twelfth*

Night, but there is no reasonable doubt that the source of the main plot of Shakespeare's play (the sub-plot is his own invention) was the *Historie of Apolonius and Silla*, taken by a certain Barnabe Rich from an Italian novel by Bandello or from its French translation, and told in English. The Italian origin of the story is of interest, for, during this period, England was greatly influenced by all forms of Italian culture, but Shakespeare's indebtedness to this particular source does not amount to more than the mere plot outline—all that gives *Twelfth Night* its humour and its romantic charm is his own.

EDITIONS OF SHAKESPEARE'S PLAYS

In Shakespeare's time it was not fashionable for a dramatist to publish his own works. It was not until seven years after his death, in 1623, that two of his fellow-actors, Heming and Condell, collected the plays in one volume, called, from its size, the *folio* edition. During his life, however, many of the plays were piratically published by booksellers, in what are known as *quarto* editions. It has been suggested that these were taken down in the theatre word for word as they were acted, but it is unlikely that, before shorthand was perfected, such a method would have been successful, and probably the publisher-bookseller (there was then no distinction between these trades) would bribe an actor to let him see a copy of the play. These quartos were sold for sixpence in St. Paul's Churchyard.

These old editions of Shakespeare's plays differ in certain ways from the more modern ones. Stage directions occur,* but there are no lists of *dramatis*

* An interesting one in *Twelfth Night* is " Enter Viola and Malvolio, at several doors " (II. ii.), indicating the construction of the stage in the older theatre.

personæ, and no headings to indicate where the various scenes are supposed to take place. Occasionally a passage of blank verse is printed as prose ; a passage of prose as verse. Sometimes the meaning of a passage is obscure, but with the correction of a more or less obvious misprint or mistake in the text it becomes clear. Other quarto and folio editions of the plays were published during the seventeenth century. In the eighteenth century the work of editing the text began. Pope, Rowe, Hanmer, Capell, Theobald, Dr. Johnson brought out editions which contain lists of *dramatis personæ*, indications of where the scene is supposed to take place, and emendations of passages where certain words or phrases appear to be corrupt. Some of these emendations have been found to be unnecessary, others have been accepted by later scholars and critics. For the chief ones made in the first folio version of *Twelfth Night* (there is no surviving quarto of this play) see pages 144–146. Students who are sufficiently advanced to be interested in text questions should examine this version at first hand where possible. There is a facsimile in the library of every big town.

CLASSICAL ALLUSION IN "TWELFTH NIGHT"

Admiration of the thoughts and achievements of the " noble Grecians and Romans " is one of the characteristics of Elizabethan culture. At no other period has there been so widespread a pleasure in and knowledge of the beautiful and stirring tales of classic myth, and the personages, human and divine, who figure in them. They are used as subjects of plays and masques ; they appear in long poem and tiny lyric ; allusions to them come naturally and easily in writing and in talk. Sometimes, of course, these allusions are dully and absurdly made, by pedants and mere followers of fashion, but generally they have a fresh and delightful beauty, and some of the loveliest imagery of Shakespeare, Marlowe, and Spenser is drawn from these myths.

You will not find so much allusion to classic myth in *Twelfth Night* as in Shakespeare's earlier plays. When Orsino wonders at Cesario's girlish appearance he says that " Diana's lip is not more smooth and rubious." Diana is the virgin goddess of hunting and the moon. One day Actæon, hunting in the woods, came to a fountain in a valley closed in with cypresses and pines. Here Diana made her toilet, and, in her anger at the intruder, she dashed water from the fountain into his face. Instantly he lost his human shape, and became a stag. His own hounds set on him, and tore him to pieces. Orsino thinks of this story when he speaks of how his passions, " like fell and cruel hounds," have pursued him since he saw Olivia first. Feste alludes to one of Mercury's least desirable attributes when he says to Olivia, " Now Mercury endow thee with leasing, for thou speakest well of fools." Mercury (Hermes), the swift messenger of the gods, was renowned for his cunning. Vulcan was the smith of the gods, and made their weapons. Orsino remembers that when he last saw Antonio his face was " besmeared as black as Vulcan in the smoke of war." When Orsino, admiring Olivia's sensibility, reflects on how she will love when the " rich golden shaft " has killed all other affections in her except that which she feels for her husband, he alludes to the gold-tipped arrows of Cupid (Eros), the little god of love. These golden arrows kindled love, but a wound with his leaden ones awoke hatred.

Elysium (see page 21) was the abode of the souls of the blest after death ; Tartarus (see page 60) the dark gulf where evil-doers were doomed to languish. When, imagining that he must be dreaming of Olivia and her graciousness to him, Sebastian cries, " Let fancy still my sense in Lethe steep," he is thinking of the river of the underworld by the cave of sleep, whose waters gave oblivion of former life to those tasting them.

Penthesilea was the queen of that race of warlike women, the Amazons, who fought for the Trojans against the Greeks in the great war described by Homer. Sir Toby, of course, calls Maria Penthesilea to tease her, as she is of small stature, as different as can be from a tall Amazon. Arion was a Greek poet (600 B.C.) concerning whom the legend is told that his music and song enchanted even the creatures of the sea, and when, during a voyage, he flung himself overboard to escape from sailors who had planned to murder him for his treasures, he was carried safely to shore by a dolphin.

ON THINKING IT OVER

FOR YOUNGER BOYS AND GIRLS

(After reading an Act, see if you have noticed and know these things.)

I

WHAT do the opening scenes tell of Orsino's desire, Olivia's vow, and Viola's plight? What does Viola resolve to do to help herself? Why is Sir Andrew staying in Olivia's house, and why is Sir Toby so anxious that he should remain there? What does Maria think of him? When you have read the whole play, you must decide whether she was a good judge of character. On what errand does Orsino send Cesario? Why is the page unwilling to undertake it? What words of the Duke's in Scene iv. must have made Viola a little anxious lest he should suspect the secret of her disguise? What private ambition has Maria? At the end of the play you will know if it is realized. Why is Olivia annoyed with Feste, and how does he succeed in restoring her to good humour with him? How does Malvolio criticize the fool? (You will see later how this criticism rankles, and in what it results.) What does Olivia consider to be Malvolio's chief fault? Does Cesario perform his errand well? Why do you think " he " is so anxious to see Olivia's face? Notice what " he " says when first she unveils—and the sincere and generous admiration of her beauty that follows. What does Olivia say to herself when she feels that she is charmed by Cesario ? Does she give a thought to her vow ?

The Duke tells his page :

" I have unclasped
To thee the book even of my secret soul."

Olivia, reproving Malvolio, says that to be generous-minded is

" To take those things for birdbolts that you deem cannon-bullets."

Malvolio, telling Olivia of Feste, says :

" I saw him put down the other day with an ordinary fool that has no more brain than a stone."

Say in your own words what each of these expressions means.

Learn by heart :

" If music be the food of love, play on—" (page 19).
" Make me a willow cabin at your gate—" (page 37).

Learn by heart the meaning of these words as used by Shakespeare, so that you will know them when you come across them in another play : Cousin, dear, humour, cunning, allow, coystrill, comfortable, non-pareil, galliard, coranto, blazon.

II

Why does Antonio hesitate to accompany Sebastian to Orsino's court, and why does he finally do so ? Notice what Viola says when Malvolio gives her the ring. How, in the closing lines of Scene i., does she describe the entanglement in which she finds herself ? How does Feste succeed in impressing Sir Andrew ? Compare his " fooling " with this character with that with which he entertains Olivia. Is Malvolio fulfilling the duties of his office in reprimanding Sir Toby ? Do you think he enjoys fault-finding ? How does Maria sum up his character ?—compare what she says with Olivia's criticism in Act I. Feste says that Orsino is very changeable—that his mind is " a very opal." What does the Duke say and do in Scene iv. which proves the truth of this ? Does he know it to be a fault of his ? Why is Fabian irritated with Malvolio ? Does Malvolio imagine Olivia to be in love with him before he finds the letter ? What little touches in his day-dream show him to be ludicrously vain and self-satisfied ? Maria invents one famous sentence in her letter—which is it ? What instructions does the letter give Malvolio ?

The Elizabethans believed that the stars influence human destiny. Did you notice that any character spoke of this influence in this Act, and in Act I ?

Explain : " bear-baiting," " with what wing the staniel checks at it," " Sowter will cry upon it," " the rascally sheep-biter," " now is the woodcock near the gin," " here comes the trout that must be caught with tickling."

Learn by heart :

" O mistress mine—" (page 44).

" Come away, come away, death—" (page 51).

" She never told her love—" (page 53).

Learn by heart the meaning of these words (as used by Shakespeare) : Baffle, complexion, favour, owe, proper, welkin, point-device, champain, gin (short for engine), fustian.

III

Olivia is the kind of person who abandons herself to present emotion. Do you remember in what way she showed her grief (quite genuine grief) at her brother's death ? Now that is forgotten in her passion for Cesario, and you will notice in Scene i. how completely she gives herself up to this. Viola's is a different nature. Look again at I. ii., and II. iv. Why does Sir Andrew make up his mind to leave Olivia's house, and how does Sir Toby persuade him to stay ? Why is Antonio anxious not to be seen in the streets of

Illyria? What does he give Sebastian, and why? What does Olivia think ails Malvolio, and what instructions does she give concerning him? How does he interpret these? How do Sir Toby and company treat him? Why does Sir Toby think it better not to deliver the challenge Sir Andrew writes? "A little thing would make me tell them how much I lack of a man." What makes poor Viola think this? And what impels Sir Andrew to say to Sir Toby, "Let him let the matter slip, and I'll give him my horse, grey Capilet"? Who puts an abrupt end to the "duel," and with what unfortunate result? What request is made of Viola, and what does she at once guess? What do Sir Toby and Fabian say of Cesario when he has left them, and what does Sir Andrew then resolve to do?

In this Act, did you come across any more allusions to Elizabethan sports, such as hawking and bearbaiting?

What did you notice as to the etiquette of the duel, with which, of course, every man in the Elizabethan theatre would be familiar? Do you remember any words used for the sword, and for the different movements of fencing?

What does Olivia mean when she tells Cesario:

"But, would you undertake another suit,
    I had rather hear you to solicit that,
    Than music from the spheres."

Learn by heart:

"O, what a deal of scorn looks beautiful—" (page 65).

Learn by heart the old meaning of these words, and show how the use of them has changed nowadays: Orchard, sad, politician, jealousy, admire.

IV

Why is Sebastian bewildered and angry at the opening of this Act? What happens to the unfortunate

Sir Andrew ?   What does Olivia discover Sir Toby in the act of doing, and with what result ?   How is the joke against Malvolio kept up, and what makes Sir Toby feel it is time to end it ?   Describe the amazement of Sebastian at the graciousness of Olivia.   What does Olivia arrange as soon as she finds Cesario, as she thinks him, pleased with her favour ?   Who was the " old Vice " about whom Feste sings ?   What does the word " grig " really mean ?

How did the Elizabethans use these words : cockney, competitor, knave ?

V

At what moment does Cesario indeed seem to be the " dissembling cub " Orsino calls " him " ?   What saves the situation for " him," and how is the happy ending of the trials of all the lovers brought about ?   How is the jest played upon Malvolio revealed to Olivia, and what compensation does she promise him ?   Describe Fabian's plea for mercy.   " Thus the whirligig of time brings in his revenges," says Feste.   What particular grudge had he against Malvolio ?   What are the last words Malvolio speaks in the play ?

What are the meanings of these words : whirligig, geck, coxcomb, minion, pavan ?

FOR OLDER STUDENTS

1. Imagine the audience of Englishmen who were gathered in the Hall of the Middle Temple to watch *Twelfth Night* acted there in February 1602.   Describe as far as you can their appearance, the type of education they would have had, their little affectations, their amusements and interests, using allusions in the comedy to illustrate your description.   Note any points in the representation of the play itself

ON THINKING IT OVER

which would mark the performance as belonging to the seventeenth century.

2. " *Twelfth Night* may fairly be estimated as the chief monument of the author's genius for comedy." (Hallam.)

" Let but Falstaffe come :
  Hall, Poines, the rest, you scarce shall have a roome,
  All is so pester'd ; let but Beatrice
  And Benedick be seene, loe, in a trice
  The Cockpit, Galleries, Boxes, all are full
  To hear Malvoglio, that cross-garter'd Gull."
                      Ingleby's *Century of Praise.*

What qualities in this comedy do you think have led to its being rated so highly—by the scholar in his study and by the plain man in the theatre ?

3. The word " comedy " occurs in many phrases in English. We speak of " romantic comedy," the " comedy of manners," a " comedy of errors," " slap-stick comedy," and so on. Discuss the significance of these various terms, and show what kinds of comedy are blended in the play of *Twelfth Night*. If you are reading Molière in your French classes, consider the difference between his comic world and that of Shake-speare.

4. " There is a certain stage of society in which people become conscious of their peculiarities and absurdities, affect to disguise what they are, and set up pretensions to what they are not. This gives rise to a corresponding style of comedy, the object of which is to detect the disguises of self-love, and to make reprisals on these preposterous assumptions of vanity, by marking the contrast between the real and the affected character as severely as possible, and denying to those, who would impose on us for what they are not, even the merit which they have. This is the comedy of artificial life, of wit and satire, such as we see it in Congreve, Wycherley, Vanbrugh, etc. To

this succeeds a state of society from which the same sort of affectation and pretence are banished by a greater knowledge of the world or by their successful exposure on the stage ; and which by neutralizing the materials of comic character, both natural and arti-ficial, leaves no comedy at all—but the *sentimental*. Such is our modern comedy.   There is a period in the progress of manners anterior to both these, in which the foibles and follies of individuals are of nature's plant-ing, not the growth of art or study ; in which they are therefore unconscious of them themselves, or care not who knows them, if they can but have their whim out ; and in which, as there is no attempt at imposition, the spectators rather receive pleasure from humouring the inclinations of the persons they laugh at, than wish to give them pain by exposing their absurdity.   This may be called the comedy of nature, and it is the comedy which we generally find in Shakespeare."

Consider Hazlitt's analysis with reference to *Twelfth Night* and other comedies you may have read, in English or any other language.   If you know and like the novels of Jane Austen, you will find special interest in Hazlitt's description of the stage comedy of the early nineteenth century, compared with that of her novels.

5. George Meredith has described various mental attitudes towards the ridiculous.

" If you detect the ridicule and your kindliness is chilled by it, you are slipping into the grasp of Satire.

" If instead of falling foul of the ridiculous person with a satiric rod, to make him writhe and shriek aloud, you prefer to sting him under a semi-caress, by which he shall in his anguish be rendered dubious whether indeed anything has hurt him, you are an engine of Irony.

" If you laugh all round him, tumble him, roll him about, deal him a smack, and drop a tear on him, own his likeness to you and yours to your neighbour, spare him as little as you shun, pity him as much as you expose, it is a spirit of Humour that is moving you.

"The Comic, which is the perceptive, is the governing spirit, awakening and giving aim to these powers of laughter, but it is not to be confounded with them: it enfolds a thinner form of them, differing from satire, in not sharply driving into the quivering sensibilities, and from humour, in not comforting them and tucking them up, or indicating a broader than the range of this bustling world to them."

(*The Idea of Comedy.*)

It is interesting when you read novels or plays dealing with what is ridiculous in human characters, institutions, etc., to consider whether the attitude of the writer is that of the satirist, the "ironeïst," or the humorist, and to see if you detect the presence of the "comic spirit."

6. Discuss the title of the play. Look at the list of Shakespeare's plays, and notice how he has named them, and which names you like best.

7. Notice the different scenes where music occurs in the play. If you know other Shakespearean comedies, compare their songs with those of *Twelfth Night*, and show how they suggest the spirit of the plays to which they belong.

8. In *Twelfth Night* there is a main plot and a sub-plot. Distinguish the two, indicating very shortly (in a couple of sentences if possible) the subject of each, and its chief characters. Then show the connection between the sub-plot and the main plot, and point out the effective contrast between them.

9. A play, like most forms of literary art, must have a beginning, a middle, and an end. These essential parts of comedy are called the *situation*, the *climax*, the *solution*, or *dénouement*. Between the beginning and the middle, the " situation " and " climax," is a gradual *complication* of matters.

Show how, at the beginning of *Twelfth Night*, the

dramatist introduces the chief personages, indicating who they are, what they are like, and in what circumstances they find themselves placed. These circumstances suggest a story to come. " How will this fadge ? " asks Viola of herself, as the complication, or entanglement, begins to weave itself. (See page 42.) What is the " this " to which she refers ? Show as briefly as you can how the complication becomes more and more intricate. Where does the climax come ? And how is the solution contrived ?

10. Who are the characters who take part in the practical joke against Malvolio, and what special grudge has each of these against him ?

11. Some people say that the pleasure underlying laughter may be traced to a sense of superiority. Does this account for the enjoyment of the practical joker ? Do you know any other plays in which Shakespeare makes use of the practical joke for the sake of laughter ? What is the drawback, if any, to this type of jesting ? Which gives you more pleasure —the jest contrived against Malvolio by Maria, or that played on Sir Andrew and Cesario by Sir Toby and Fabian ?

12. With regard to the fooling of Malvolio, consider the following critical passages :

(a) " I do not wish, as Coleridge said, to flounder-flat a humorous image, but there is no evading certain results of the genuinely humanistic as opposed to the entirely humoristic rendering of certain of Shakespeare's characters. The gaunt and sombre steward is not, and is not likely to be, a purely amusing character. Even his tormentors at one point relent a little at the thought that they may carry their cruel joke too far,* and for the nineteenth century it is carried too far to be entirely funny. Malvolio in the dark hole uttering sage, conscientious words to prove

---

* From pity ? See IV. ii.

to the false Sir Topas that he is not mad, becomes a pathetic figure." (Russell.)

(*b*) " He has no sense of humour—that is the head and front of his offending. That his punishment, strictly considered, is excessive, to the point of barbarity, cannot, I think, be doubted ; but the air of the fairy tale interpenetrates the farce, and we do not demand a strict apportionment of justice either poetical or practical." (William Archer.)

(Both these passages refer to the representation of the Malvolio scenes on the stage.)

13. Is all the entertainment of the famous " letter scene " derived from the spectacle of Malvolio's illusion ? If anything else strikes you as amusing, write an appreciation of the humour of it.

14. Contrast is one of the oldest devices of dramatic entertainment. It may be the crude contrast of physical appearance and obvious personal mannerism, or the subtler difference of character. Think of where this contrast has appeared in plays you have seen in the theatre—from the pantomime upwards, and where it has seemed interesting and significant. Then illustrate Shakespeare's different uses of it in *Twelfth Night*.

15. In mediæval days, when the community of castle or hall was largely dependent on itself for its entertainment, the fool was an essential part of the great household. The history of his evolution is a fascinating one. At first he seems a sad little figure, bandy-legged and hump-backed, his peculiarities exaggerated by his gay motley dress, hung with bells. Mental and physical abnormality in themselves were entertaining to our ancestors, and the first fools were probably the objects of cruel mirth and derision. But gradually this changed. The court fool became a most privileged person, and had every opportunity of exercising the malicious wit that very often accompanies deformity of person. Jaques, in *As You Like It*, declares he envies him his liberty of criticism

(II. vii.), which may be made without fear of retaliation, as the man who shows himself sensitive to the gibes of a fool himself appears foolish. He might, of course, go too far. " Take heed, sirrah, the whip ! " Lear warns his fool when he cannot endure his allusions to the dominance of Goneril and Regan. But he dared much, in pranks as well as jests.

By the sixteenth century fooling has become a profession. Those who undertook it were by no means deficient in normal wit, nor necessarily had they any physical peculiarity, though a comical face or shape or gesture was an asset, as to a favourite modern " funny man " jesting to his huge audience from the music-hall or pantomime stage. To sing a song, improvise doggerel sententious speech, chop logic, make pithy allusion and pointed comment—all these were part of the regular stock-in-trade of the fool. His task needed tact and discretion—Viola, you will remember, is struck with its difficulties (*Twelfth Night*, III. i.). Feste is able to cope with all these—he is the cleverest (and the least wise) of Shakespeare's three famous fools. Study his skill, with reference to Viola's description of what the qualities of the fool should be, and, if you have read or seen the plays to which they belong, compare him with Touchstone and Lear's fool.

16. Often Shakespeare studies the same type of character in two different plays. If you have read or seen *Henry IV.* and *Romeo and Juliet*, compare Falstaff with Sir Toby, Orsino with Romeo. Do not try to work out this comparison unless you know these plays at first hand and not merely through being told about them. Such comparisons are interesting only if you have, as it were, met the characters yourself.

17. If you know Rosalind, Portia, Beatrice, as well as Viola, write a study of Shakespeare's girls. The story of the play must make its own kind of heroine, but you will find that these young women have certain

points in common — they are stamped as Shakespeare's. Bring out both their resemblance to one another and their individual personalities in your appreciation.

18. Hallam, discussing Viola, says that she " would be more interesting if she had not indelicately, as well as unfairly towards Olivia, determined to win the Duke's heart before she had seen him." Gervinus talks of Olivia's " proneness to go to extremes." Halliwell describes Sir Andrew as " always enjoying a joke, and never understanding it." Test the justice of these critical remarks by reference to the play.

19. It is useless for a dramatist to give a complete and detailed description of the appearance of his men and women, as they are to live on the stage through actors and actresses, but, like every creator absorbed in his characters, Shakespeare occasionally gives descriptive touches as to personal appearance, voice, demeanour—we know that Portia is golden-haired, Rosalind and Helena are tall, Cordelia has a low and gentle voice, Lear is every inch a king, and so on. Have you noticed any such descriptive touches with regard to the persons in *Twelfth Night ?*

20. What do you know of the various athletic exercises, sports, or amusements referred to in the following passages :

(*a*) Look you now, he's out of his guard already.

(*b*) He's a coward and a coystrill that will not drink to my niece till his brains turn o' the toe like a parish-top.

(*c*) He brought me out of favour with my lady about a bear-baiting here.

(*d*) With what wing the staniel checks at it !

(*e*) Shall I play my freedom at tray-trip ?

(*f*) Like to the old Vice
Who, with dagger of lath,
In his rage and his wrath,

Cries ah, ha ! to the devil.

(g) Nature to her bias drew in that.

21. To what ancient ideas and beliefs are allusions made in the following passages :

(a) Were we not born under Taurus ?

(b) I know thy constellation is right apt
For this affair.

(c) 'Tis not the time of the moon with me to make one in so skipping a dialogue.

(d) Does not our life consist of the four elements ? (Cf. I am not of your element.)

(e) I had rather hear you to solicit that
Than music from the spheres.

(f) What is the opinion of Pythagoras concerning wildfowl ?

22. The Elizabethans were as much interested in conversational style and brilliance as they were in the intricate fashion and splendid colouring of their clothes. Theirs is a wonderful period for beauty and pith of phrase—there are treasures of expression in both sonnet of sad true love and slangy prose pamphlet. It is inevitable that a good deal of affectation in speech should occur at a time when preoccupation with words is general. Shakespeare, his ear sensitive to every turn of talk as that of a musician to different harmonies, was interested in all word fashions, and most of his plays have some allusion to them. Read the opening of Viola's " prepared speech " to Olivia in I. v., and compare the loveliness of her unrehearsed emotional expression in the " 'Tis beauty truly blent " and " Make me a willow cabin " passages. Notice how Sir Toby blossoms into courtierly affectation when talking to Cesario in III. i., and how much impressed Sir Andrew is with the same Cesario's greeting of Olivia. Notice, too, Viola and Feste's discussion of words.

23. Do you remember any words in this play connected with sport and games—hunting, hawking,

bear-baiting, bowls, fencing, etc. ? Are any of these in common modern use ?

24. Have you noticed any words derived from the Italian and Spanish languages ? Do you know why it was likely that a certain amount of these should come into our language at this time ?

25. If you are studying the history of language—

(*a*) Distinguish between the different usages of the following words in Elizabethan and in modern English : Cousin, delivered, estate, dear, humour, codling (quodling), cunning, comfortable, allow, baffle, favour, owe, complexion, proper, spinster, free, orchard, prevented, sad, sonnet, politician, jealousy, admire, opposite, advise, abuse, cockney, competitor, discourse, knave, enlarge, delivers, shrewdly, fancy.

(*b*) Look up the derivation and notice the meaning of these words—Buttery-bar, cloistress, masques, coranto, kickshaws, coystrill, galliard, crowner (coroner), zany, ducat, sinister, grain, blazon, motley, canton, viol-de-gamboys, nonpareil, beshrew, champain, cozier, cypress, damask, fustian, gin, jet, malignancy, sack, taffetas, testril, welkin, Sophy, point-device, bawcock, cheveril, duello, grize, hob, nob, orchard, renegade, stuck, tuck, yare, maugre, barricade, clerestory, shent, malapert, bias, coxcomb, geck, interlude, let, lullaby, minion, othergates, pavan, bawbling.

(Keep a special book for your words, and you will soon have an interesting little etymological dictionary of your own.)

26. The following are emendations of various passages in the first or other folios by Shakespearean editors. Would you reject any of these ? Show why those which seem entirely satisfactory have been made. (Consult the context of the passage in every case.)

TWELFTH NIGHT

FOLIOS	EMENDATIONS
I. i., page 19. . . . like the sweet *sound* That breathes upon a bank of violets.	. . . like the sweet *south* . . . (Pope).
I. ii., page 21. Like *Orion* on the dol- phin's back.	. . . *Arion* . . . (Pope).
I. iii., page 24. Castiliano *vulgo* !	Castiliano *volto* ! (Theo- bald).
I. iii., page 26. It will not *coole my* nature.	It will not *curl by* nature (Theobald).
I. iii., page 27. 'Tis strong and does in- different well in a *dam'd- coloured* stock.	'Tis . . . a *flame-coloured* stock (Rowe). . . . a *damask-coloured* stock (Knight).
I. v., page 29. A good *lenton* answer.	A good *lenten* answer (Rowe).
II. i., page 41. I could not with such es- timable wonder overfar believe that.	I could not with such *an* estimable wonder over- far believe that (Wil- liams).
II. ii., page 42. She took *the* ring of me : I'll none of it.	She took *no* ring of me . . . (Malone, etc.).
II. iii., page 43. *Deluculo* surgere.	*Diluculo* surgere (Rowe).
II. iii., page 43. *Does* not our *lives* consist of the four elements ?	*Do* . . . elements ? (Malone, etc.). *Does* . . . *life* . . . elements ? (Rowe).
II. iii., page 44. I sent thee sixpence for thy *lemon*.	I sent thee sixpence for thy *leman* (Theobald).

Castiliano volto, " Put on your Castilian countenance," *i.e.*
grave, solemn looks.

ON THINKING IT OVER

II. iii., page 49.
That old and *antic* song we heard last night.

That . . . *antique* song . . . night (Pope).

II. v., page 57.
With what wing the *stallion* checks at it.

With . . . *staniel* . . . **it** (Hanmer).

III. i., page 62.
Fools are as like to husbands as *pilchers* to herrings.

Fools . . . *pilchards* to herrings (Capell).

III. i., page 63.
But *wisemens folly fallen*, quite taint their wit.

But *wise men, folly-fallen*, quite taint their wit (Capell).

III. iii., page 69.
I can no other answer make, but thanks

I . . . make, but thanks And thanks, *and ever thanks ; and oft* good turns (Theobald, etc.).

And thanks : *and ever oft* good turns.

I . . . thanks And . . . thanks ; *too* oft good turns (Seymour, etc.).

III. iv., page 77.
Goes on my master's *griefs*.

Goes . . . *grief* (Rowe).

IV. ii., page 90.
Adieu, goodman *devil !*

Adieu, goodman, *drivel !* (Rowe).

27. Compare the readings of these passages in Folio 1 and one or all of the later Folios :

FOLIO 1   OTHER FOLIOS

II. v., page 54.
How now, my *mettle* of India !

How now, my *nettle* of India ! (F. 2).

III. iv., page 73.
Let thy tongue *langer* with arguments of state.

Let . . . *tang* . . . state (F. 2, 3, 4).

III. iv., page 78.
His indignation derives itself out of a very *computent* injury.

His . . . *competent* injury (F. 2, 3, 4).

145

IV. iii., page 92.

My most *iealious* and too doubtful soul.	My most *jealous* . . . soul (F. 2, 3, 4).

28. What scenes in this play are written in prose ? If you have read other plays by Shakespeare, look at them again, and notice for what type of scene prose is invariably used.

29. In beginning to read Shakespeare the scansion of blank verse should be studied, at first in its simplest form, then with its variations. This should be done gradually—on one day a few perfectly regular lines, on the next lines with a trochaic first foot, and so on. From time to time a verse passage set down as prose should be re-written in its blank verse lines. Those who have a good ear for poetry read at once with observance of the harmony of blank verse ; a slight over-emphasis of the rhythm will help those who do not easily detect it. From the earliest stages lines in which the sound echoes the sense with particular distinctness should be noticed, and attention called to the effect of long and short vowel sounds, liquid, sibilant, guttural, and explosive consonants.

30. Coleridge thus describes the speaking of

" A blank, my lord ; she never told her love !—
But let concealment," etc.

" After the first line (of which the last five words should be spoken with, and drop down in, a deep sigh) the actress ought to make a pause ; and then start afresh, from the activity of thought, born of suppressed feelings, and which thought had accumulated during the brief interval, as vital heat under the skin during a dip in cold water."

Take any passage or scene which has specially interested you in the reading of the play, and describe the way in which you think it ought to be spoken, and with what action it should be accompanied on the stage.

ON THINKING IT OVER

31. (a) It seems to have been usual at one time to act Viola in such a way as to emphasize the pathos of her situation. Miss Ellen Terry, in the nineteenth century, "modified the sentimentality" of former renderings, and played the part gaily, and so did Miss Neilson. Miss Ada Rehan represented her as "a woman of deep sensibility, permitting a wistful sadness to glimmer through the gauze of kindly vivacity with which, otherwise, her bright and gentle figure is artfully swathed." What scenes justify this wistful and pathetic rendering, and where, on the other hand, has Viola some of the gay swagger of Rosalind? How would you like to see her played?

(b) In a recent representation of *Twelfth Night* the actor playing Feste could not sing, and a gentleman attending Olivia was called upon to sing his songs. Do you think this a tolerable innovation?

(c) What do you think of these renderings of Malvolio:—

"Bensley threw over the part an air of Spanish loftiness. He looked, spake, and moved like an old Castilian. He was starch, spruce, opinionated, but his superstructure of pride seemed bottomed upon a sense of worth. . . . He was magnificent from the outset; but when the decent sobrieties of the character began to give way, and the poison of self-love, in his conceit of the Countess's affection, gradually to work, you would have thought that the hero of La Mancha in person stood before you. How he went smiling to himself! With what ineffable carelessness would he twirl his gold chain! What a dream it was! You were infected with the illusion, and did not wish that it should be removed. You had no room for laughter. You felt that an hour of such mistake was worth an age with the eyes open. Who would not wish to live but for a day in the conceit of such a lady's love as

The hero of La Mancha, Don Quixote.

Olivia ? Why, the Duke would have given his princi-
pality for a quarter of a minute, sleeping or waking, to
have been so deluded. . . . I confess that I never saw
the catastrophe of this character, while Bensley played
it, without a kind of tragic interest " (Lamb).

" Lean, lank, with self-occupied visage and formal,
peaked Spanish beard ; dressed in close garb of black
striped with yellow, and holding a steward's wand, in
the lightness of which there is something of fantastic
symbolism, Irving steps on the stage with nose in
air and eyes half shut, as if with singular and moody
contemplation. He is visibly possessed of pride, of
manners, and of intelligence. His pride, though
intense, is not diseased, until the poison-dish of
imagined love has been presented to him and has
begun its work. Irving's gait ; his abstraction of
gaze, qualified by a polite observance of his lady, and
a suspicious vigilance over his fellows in her service
and her turbulent relations and followers ; his sublime
encounter with the Fool ; his sententious observations
on everything in general, and the infinite gravity yet
imaginative airiness of his movements, carry the Malvolio of Shakespeare to a higher point of effect, probably, than it has ever before reached on the stage "
(Russell).

32. If you see *Twelfth Night* acted, notice any re-
arrangement of scenes, explain why the modern stage
manager has thought this necessary, and decide if you
agree with him. Which scenes gain by representation
on the stage, and which, if any, lose ? Perhaps, during a Shakespearean season in the town where you live,
you will see both a play you have studied and one that
is quite new to you. If so, does foreknowledge increase or diminish the enjoyment of Shakespearean
drama ?

33. There are many ways of representing Shakespearean plays. Originally they were acted on an
apron stage without scenery, as we understand the

term (see page 110). The idea of reproducing the costume of the period to which the events of the play belong is a comparatively modern one (see pages 12, 110). In the eighteenth century Viola and Sebastian appeared in laced coats and perruques, and Olivia was like a lady of the court of Queen Anne in her powder and patches. In the nineteenth century, stage managers like Kean and Tree attempted the most elaborate and detailed realism in scenery and dress. Then Gordon Craig inaugurated a new way, designing settings which should suggest to the imagination the spirit and atmosphere of the tragedy or comedy, instead of showing the eye a multitude of realistic touches, which, correct enough in their way, may quite well fail in their purpose, and prove tiresome and absurd. (" I let my scenes grow out of not merely the play, but from broad sweeps of thought which the play has conjured up in me."—*The Art of the Theatre*, Gordon Craig, page 29.) In the modern theatre you may see a Shakespearean play staged very simply against a curtained background, or realistically, or in the imaginative way suggested by Gordon Craig. The very latest notion has been to return to the old custom of disregarding period, and to play *Cymbeline* and *Hamlet* in modern dress—and with more modern accessories than in the eighteenth century, when it was not necessary to substitute an automatic pistol for a rapier !

Discuss these various ways of showing a Shakespearean play and discover which you consider the most satisfying to the imagination. If you have skill in drawing, plan out designs for scenes and costumes for *Twelfth Night*, bearing in mind the practical necessity of economy in scene-shifting and dress-changing in the theatre.

34. From time to time, for the sake of testing your understanding of what you read, you should try to express a short passage of the play you are studying

in modern prose. Every one knows, of course, that part of the meaning is bound up in the form, that you cannot get the *value* of the original passage in another rendering, but this exercise of paraphrasing does prove if you are reading with intelligence. In giving the gist of the following passages do not necessarily *reproduce* the explanation of word or phrase given in the footnotes, for this is a mere explanation, and might fit in clumsily with your rendering.

In Act I. try :

Page 19. " Nought . . . minute."
  ,,   22. " O that . . . estate is."
  ,,   24. " He hath the gift . . . grave."
  ,,   28. " You either fear . . . love."
  ,,   31. " Doth he not . . . fool."
  ,,   35. " I am . . . usage."
  ,,   38. " I . . . post."

In Act II. :

Page 40. " The malignancy . . . yours."
  ,,   40. " My determinate . . . extravagancy."
  ,,   41. " I could not . . . that."
  ,,   48. " An affectioned . . . work."

In Act III. :

Page 69. " I can no answer make . . . dealing."
  ,,   76. " It comes to pass . . . him."
  ,,   78. " His indignation . . . desire."
  ,,   82. " I'll lend . . . you."
  ,,   82. " Is't possible . . . persuasion ? "

In Act IV. :

Page 88. " I would we were . . . upshot.'
  ,,   91. " His counsel now . . . mad."

In Act V. :

Page 95. " A bawbling . . . honour on him."
  ,,   95. " His false cunning . . . wink."
  ,,   98. " Alas . . . propriety."
  ,, 105. " Most freely . . . against."

ON THINKING IT OVER

35. Orsino, like King Richard II., is sometimes described as a study in what is called the "artistic temperament." What is meant by this phrase? How far is the common use of it justifiable? Study Orsino as an artist in sensation, and compare him with Olivia in this respect.

36. It is sometimes said that Shakespeare has satirized Puritanism in the figure of Malvolio. Where are allusions made to his Puritanism? Do you know why there was no love lost between those who were in any way connected with the stage and the Puritans? Does Malvolio seem to you a satirical study of a typical member of this sect?

37. When his company played at the houses of English noblemen, Shakespeare would have come into personal contact with the steward or seneschal, for it would be the latter's business to provide accommodation for the actors, and sometimes to arrange what entertainment they should give. Make a little one-act play on an imaginary episode in the country house of a nobleman of the Elizabethan period, in which a steward and Will Shakespeare are the chief characters, and let it end with the flash into Shakespeare's mind that out of this "time-pleaser," this "affectioned ass," he will make—Malvolio.

The names of some of the actors in the company to which Shakespeare belonged were Richard Burbage (the tragedian), Lawrence Fletcher, Augustine Phillips, John Heming and Henry Condell (who were to publish the First Folio after Shakespeare's death), William Kemp (the actor of Peter and Falstaff), and William Sly.

38. There has been much diversity of opinion as to the merits of Feste's last song. Some critics have called it "wretched stuff," "an old song, scarcely worth correction," a "nonsensical ditty," and have considered that Shakespeare had nothing to do with it, but that it was part of the clown's "jig" (see page 106), and was tacked on to the play in the actors'

copy from which Heming and Condell printed their Folio edition of the plays. Knight, on the other hand, says : "We hold this song to be the most philosophical clown's song upon record : and a treatise might be written upon its wisdom. It is the history of a life, from the condition of ' a little tiny boy,' through ' man's estate,' to decaying age,—' when I come unto my bed '—and the conclusion is, that what is true of the individual is true of the species, and what was of yesterday was of generations long past away, for ' A great while ago the world begun.' "

How does this song appeal to you ?

Printed in Great Britain by
Thomas Nelson and Sons Ltd, Edinburgh